AF483604

YOUR COMPETITIVE ADVANTAGE IN BUSINESS

LEADING

with

EMOTIONAL

INTELLIGENCE

IN THE AGE OF AUTOMATION, ROBOTICS & AI

KEVIN MANN

To my incredible, emotionally resilient family.

And, with heartfelt thanks for their interviews and valuable insights:

Dr. George Lindenfeld, Mayor Paul Volker, Carolyn Taylor,

Naveen Jain, Larry DeWitt, Craig Edland, Shep Hyken,

Melody Brooke, Ishwar Joshi, Michele Grimaldi,

Albert Mensah, and Leonard Lynskey.

Continue the leadership journey at:

www.LeadingWithEQ.com

Contents

Foreword

As I first read the manuscript of *Leading with Emotional Intelligence*, I recognized this is a breakthrough book for leadership and business. The message, tools and techniques described in this book are more relevant than ever.

I work with executives, leaders, and business owners to build loyal relationships with their customers and employees. My focus is on delivering amazing customer service, customer engagement, managing the customer experience, and creating customer loyalty. I have spent many years writing, mentoring, and presenting similar ideas. As I read through the manuscript, I found myself motivated and influenced by this material - exploring new perspectives and applications.

I have always recognized that building an emotional connection is important to the customer experience. To create a rich customer service and experience culture from the top-down, leaders must develop values and vision that they can share internally and externally.

I have known Kevin Mann as a peer author and technology executive who is well informed in all the aspects of business. From my interaction with him on customer service, relationship building, and stakeholder engagement, he has fresh and innovative ideas on systemizing relationship building with modern digital and AI tools.

Emotional intelligence and the concept of *Deliberate Leadership* belong together. As we know, emotional intelligence refers to the ability to perceive, evaluate, and respond to emotions. Emotional intelligence is not an innate ability but a learnable skill that is especially valuable in the workplace. The workplace is a unique melting pot of people with different skills, knowledge, personalities, emotions, and levels of personal awareness. A deliberate leader with emotional intelligence can assess customers,' employees,' or stakeholders' feelings and act accordingly — whether to de-escalate confrontations, improve production, or inspire confidence. Kevin Mann presents scientifically proven ways to harness the power of emotional intelligence that helps eliminate customer dissatisfaction and can transition more of your customers from "satisfied" to "loyal." *Leading with Emotional Intelligence* provides practical tools on how to do that.

This is not a business or leadership book with just theories and ideological examples. This material is practical and demonstrates how leaders can leverage their emotional intelligence to tap into their most valuable resource—people – and how they can inspire those people to revamp the organization's process to align with its core values. In the rapidly changing business world that often adds stress due to a rising complex business environment and advancement of technologies, nourishing our relationship is more critical than ever before.

This book offers processes, tools, and techniques to help find better solutions to our complex business problems. This book goes deeper and broader into relevant business topics like - relationship building, influencing mindsets without positional power, change & crisis management, and more. You will learn to manage complex business situations where the stakes are notoriously high, and emotions run strong. This book also shows a practical approach to building a well-rounded leader with a healthy body, mind, and soul.

Here you will discover how to harness the principles of deliberate leadership paired with your aptitude in a way that promotes adaptive "EQ" (Emotional Quotient) from top to bottom. How your business can leverage that combined "EQ" in the areas of customer service, customer experience, employees' retention, and stakeholder engagement is a core theme of this book.

I encourage you to dig into this material, pause, and think about each part. Apply what you have learned, and then go back to this book and learn more. I write this with my best wishes that *Leading with Emotional Intelligence* will inspire and influence great leaders for many years to come.

Happy Reading!

Shep Hyken, customer service/experience expert and *New York Times* bestselling author

Chapter 1

Introduction—How Did We Get Here?

"The measure of intelligence is the ability to change."

—Albert Einstein

You picked up this book for a good reason. Perhaps you're a business owner who wants to motivate your team to solve your customers' most challenging problems. Perhaps you're managing a particular group that has high employee turnover or has consistently shown low productivity. Maybe you're unsure how well contractors and vendors are supporting your most demanding customers. Whatever your reason, this book has proven, time-tested techniques to help you manage your team, engage stakeholders or oversee operations, marketing, customer service, and much more.

Let's face it: being a leader in today's business world, and in this complex digital age, is far from straightforward. Fortunately, great leaders like you aren't just born—they're made. Personality and charisma can help, but behavior makes a great leader, and behavior can be learned. Managing human behavior and understanding emotions are critical for the sustained success of any business. Leading deliberately and intelligently is key to unlocking an organization's true potential. This can be achieved only by building trust, facilitating relationships, and fostering collaboration.

Your feelings, passion, and energy can help you accomplish your goals. But what is necessary for every successful leader to understand is how other people feel, what makes them passionate, and how to channel their energies for the organization's good. Because, as a leader, you enable others to act. In this book, I'll provide you with a collection of practical and easy-to-follow business and leadership advice relevant to this uniquely challenging age.

We are living through a fast-paced, ever-changing revolution of robotics, automation, and AI. At the same time, there's an equally fast-paced and groundbreaking "evolution" in the human skills and abilities required to make these technological changes possible. What a "revolutionized" work industry means for today's leadership challenges is the purpose of this book. Over the past few decades, we went from *physically managing* machines to *intelligently leading* people. Now we are facing the potential of virtually managing robots and AI along with complex human elements. *In an age in which it seems everything is changing, the timeless skills described in this book are more relevant than ever before.*

You might be familiar with the term "Emotional Intelligence." In recent years, this term has come into vogue throughout the business community, and many books have been written on the subject. This book is not a comprehensive Emotional Intelligence or Organizational Psychology book. If you are looking for that, there are a myriad of articles and books published on this subject. This book captures lessons learned from interviews I've had with C-level executives, managers, self-made billionaires, mayors, and scientists over the last several years and draws upon research in neuroscience, organizational psychology, and real-world studies. This book will teach you how to harness the principles of Emotional Intelligence and Deliberate Leadership that promote an adaptive environment from top to bottom in today's digital age in ways that will directly impact your company's P&L statement. It will explain how you can transform your leadership style to grow and retain your customers, reduce employee turnover, and engage stakeholders for the greater good.

How intentional are you in your behavior and setting the right tone for your organization? Are you self-aware and conscious about the impact your decision can make in your business? Deliberate leadership is about embracing your business's core values to influence your groups or stakeholders' behavior for the greater good. Combine this with emotional intelligence, understanding how *other people* feel, what makes *them* passionate, and channel *their* energies for the organization's interest.

Answers to the Most Common Business Problems

A crucial aspect of leading is working with and managing a variety of personalities in various situations. As research has shown, the vast majority of leaders have a narrow understanding of human behavior and core motivation principles. For instance, do you know how empathy can give you a competitive edge in business and when to reject it politely? Do you know how to empower your salesforce for strategic or complex sales who comes from a transactional sales environment? These questions and the ones that follow are some of the most pressing in business and workplace today, and I will answer them in this book.

- How do you manage a team without positional authority?
- How can you influence the mindset of employees who may be reluctant to share your vision?
- When should you make an emotional appeal in complex or strategic sales, and when is an appeal to reason more effective?
- How can you lead your team through change while overcoming resistance?
- Often, customers insist you implement their ideas even when your experience says otherwise. How can you dissuade them from pursuing an unfeasible idea and guide them to a more advantageous outcome?
- Given that 70% of employees report disengagement at work, what practical measures can you take to improve their team's focus and productivity?
- An alarming number of C-level executives suffer from "CEO Disease," which happens when they lose touch with how their business is perceived. How can you prevent this from happening in your organization?
- If you are repeatedly underestimated, second-guessed, or misjudged in the office, it might not simply be "bad luck." What actions can you take to gain or retain your status?
- What customer retention challenges business commonly face,

and how can you overcome them?

- Why do successful companies that have merged or been acquired fail to reach their strategic and financial goals?

- What drives human behavior in a crisis? How can you manage your team in the aftermath of a disaster or after significant business events?

- What has modern neuroscience revealed about the human mind, and how is that information relevant to you as a business leader?

- With the increased use of AI, automation, and robotics, how can managers and leaders make themselves indispensable in their company and drive innovation?

The techniques provided here are helpful for every type of leader and organization, from the government sector to commercial enterprises, from small businesses to large corporations.

The Evolution of Intelligence in Business

Just as change is constant, the concept of intelligence in business and leadership has evolved over the years. Consequently, the workforce system has evolved to focus on developing and retaining knowledgeable workers. Through the ages, people have been developing more productive and efficient ways to work.

Let's go back to the 18th century, during the **First Industrial Revolution**. Europe and the United States were seeing a transition from hand production to innovative and mechanized production in the workplace.

In 1870, the **Second Industrial Revolution**, also known as the Technological Revolution, saw the introduction of mass production with the help of electrical power. This period also saw the invention of the Bessemer process to produce steel. By the early 20th century, Henry Ford's company mass-produced the groundbreaking Model T car.

Before we fast forward 150 years, let's consider the rapid industrialization of the economy in these two periods that cost many manual and craft workers their jobs. For example, in the textile industry—where the impact was most substantial and immediate—many weavers were suddenly unemployed since they could not compete with machines that only required relatively limited (and unskilled) labor to produce more cloth than a single weaver could ever produce. Many such unemployed weavers and other workers turned their hatred towards the machines that had taken their jobs and began destroying factories and machinery. This rapid industrialization turned the workers to despise machines.

Following management theories, models, and practices developed over 150 years, employees and managers were working hard in factories, and when they failed to achieve their desired results, the solution was to work harder. This led to burnout, misunderstandings, and lack of support from their teams, management, and boards.

The **Third Industrial Revolution**, or the Digital Revolution, started in the 1950s when the American economy showed strong resilience after World War II and the great depression. This period leveraged electronics and IT to automate production. As retail, manufacturing, healthcare, and transportation were digitized in these decades, the wave of technological change washed over virtually every business. Several remarkable technologies emerged, from efficient software to more dexterous robots, from novel materials to new industrial processes and a range of web-based services. Many revolutionary leadership and management approaches emerged in this era. "The Toyota Way" principles became very popular in the manufacturing industry. Many companies begin to systematically explore the alternatives of splitting up their processes of production, thus creating "offshore sourcing" which got picked up in the wind of globalization. Corporations slowly started to reengineer the management and created a horizontal rather than a hierarchical organization. These widely adopted organizational principles changed the future of leadership forever and became the foundation of the management we see in most companies today. In 1989, the World Wide Web (WWW) was invented by Tim Berners-Lee and Robert Cailliau. Two years later, in 1991, when the World Wide Web became publicly available, that gave birth to a new technology that changed the world as we knew it.

Today we are in the **Fourth Industrial Revolution.** Past innovations and the adoption of digital technologies are being used to advance physical and biological systems. Technologies like the Internet of Things (IoT), 5G, and Blockchain are enabling rapid changes affecting every discipline, industry, and economy.

Evolution of Leadership Intelligence since the Industrial Revolution

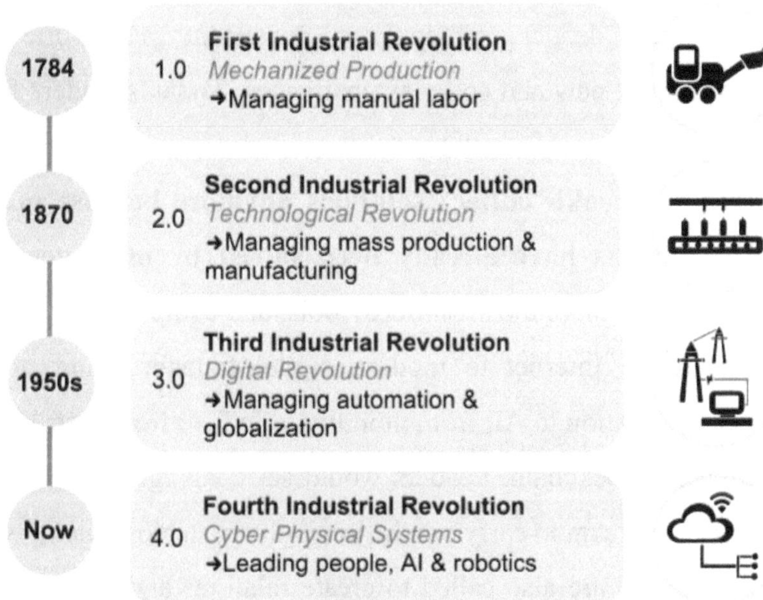

We've adapted to these changes, and now our focus has switched from the body to the mind. Physical strength is less significant, whereas mental strength, knowledge, and skills are more valuable. As I mentioned earlier, we have gone from physically managing machines to more intelligently leading people.

Now we are facing the potential of virtually managing robots and AI as we concurrently lead people. We are living through a fast-paced, ever-changing revolution of robotics, automation, and AI. At the same time, there's an equally fast-paced and groundbreaking "evolution" in the skills and abilities required to make these technological changes possible.

The rules of the game in business have changed so quickly that many haven't even noticed. Companies face more performance requirements than they did 20 years ago. Widespread structural changes require leaders to apply a consistent people-oriented approach to meet new and complex challenges. Today's leaders face unique problem-solving challenges. These challenges are new in that **there are no "cookie-cutter" solutions anymore because many tactical problems have already been solved by machines**. By "machines", I mean all the inventions, tools, and equipment available today, from the Internet to modern digital transformation, from computer automation to AI, from mobility to IoT, or from distributed computing to Blockchain. Leaders would set goals, give directions, and expect their team to carry out the job in the past. Now, along with all those, leaders are also called to create relations and connections and align common goals.

Emotions Drive Business

When you hear the word "emotion" what comes to mind? We might think of feelings like joy, sadness, fear, anger, or disgust. We might think of the highest highs and the lowest lows. Given this dramatic conception of emotions, it's perhaps no surprise that, as a society, we tend to avoid talking about emotions. In business, "emotion" was once considered a weakness, and it was a laughable topic. Today, we all know the power of understanding, acknowledging, and supporting people's emotions in workplace and business.

The word "emotion" was adapted from the French word *émouvoir* in 1579, which means "to stir up." With nothing to agitate or cause anxiety, the mind is tranquil, calm, and peaceful, like a pond with no ripples. If you throw a stone into the pond or blow into a glass of water, you will see the ripple effect in concentric circles. Since 60% of the human body comprises fluid, and we know fluid is vulnerable to external stimuli. Our bodies and minds are frequently "stirred up" by the outside world.

The emotional connection between managers and employees is key to motivation and retainment. It's necessary to have skills that go beyond hiring, placing, and training.

Whether big or small, private or public, government or commercial, all businesses need leaders who can navigate their teams through change. Recent technological advances, such as digitization, the adoption of AI, and the spread of mobile technologies, influence the speed at which social and economic changes occur. This is most evident in the business world. As a leader, you are accountable for your company's growth and the success and livelihood of your employees. Every decision you make and each action you take impacts a large and diverse community. Regardless of your leadership style, you are expected to make sustainable decisions that consider all stakeholders' interests—employees, clients, suppliers, shareholders, and the community.

As you think that increasing business complexity and rapid changes are problematic, you're right. But they also offer tremendous opportunities. Tap into those opportunities by effectively managing the emotions that result from these changes. Then channel those emotions in such a way that can make your organization successful. We'll discuss this and more.

So, what is Emotional Intelligence, and why is it relevant in leadership?

Emotional Intelligence is the ability to accurately discern one's own emotions and those of others and use this understanding to improve the workplace, guide thinking, and motivate behavioral changes. Self-awareness is the foundation of Emotional Intelligence and Deliberate Leadership. Knowing who you are and what your business or team needs is both an art and a science. Undeniably, you have to understand your emotions consciously before you can understand the emotions of others. Those who are able to understand the feelings of others can help channel these emotions in the most positive direction. Additionally, studies have shown that people with high degrees of Emotional Intelligence have better mental health, do their jobs better, and go above and beyond to improve the bottom line.

While we may think we know a lot about Emotional Intelligence, according to an article published in *Harvard Business Review*, EQ scores rise as executives climb the organizational ladder, they peak at the manager level, they fall off after that, eventually bottoming out at the CEO level. According to a Gallup poll, only 18% of managers in the United States have a talent for leadership skills, including the ability to encourage accountability in the workplace, motivate workers, and build relationships. It's no surprise, and the results speak for themselves — 68% of employees are disengaged. I would argue this is due to the shortcomings of managers. And I believe it all stems from a lack of Emotional Intelligence and Deliberate Leadership. Gallup estimates this lack of employee engagement costs the US economy about half a trillion dollars in lost productivity every year. This cost to a single company can be the difference between a business's success or failure. **The cost of employee separation (or employee turnover) is at least 20% of the employee's annual salary, reducing company profit.** In the information economy, the stakes are even higher. When your employee leaves, they not only take critical business information with them, but they also take that knowledge to one of your competitors. It's a double-edged sword. This is both an economic and an emotional crisis that has profound implications for every business.

Let's look at two major forms of intelligence. We use both cognitive intelligence (measured by IQ) and Emotional Intelligence (measured by EQ) to lead our teams. Cognitive intelligence helps in problem-solving, whereas Emotional Intelligence allows us to harness solutions through rational decision-making. Likewise, cognitive intelligence helps us retain information. Emotional Intelligence gives us the language and tone to communicate so we can influence others and impact the business and the community we live in. Just as Intelligence Quotient (IQ) measures an individual's intelligence, Emotional Quotient (EQ) assesses Emotional Intelligence. IQ is used to determine an individual's cognitive abilities, and EQ is defined as one's ability to identify, control, and manage emotions.

Cognitive Intelligence - IQ	Emotional Intelligence - EQ
Learning	Forming abstract concepts
Comprehending	Maintaining logical reasoning
Problem Solving	Planning & Decision Making
Retaining Information	Communicating & Influencing

Having higher EQ is important for effective leadership, management, customer service, sales & marketing staff, and HR. It helps them promote team effort, communicate better, and make sound decision making. On the flip side, having low EQ can contribute to high employee turnover and customer churn.

When the stakes are high, emotions run strong, and the stakeholders show resistance, the success of your business depends more on your and your executives' EQ – more than IQ and knowledge of the subject matter. **This is more vital at the top, where business issues grow more complex and the stakes become notoriously high.** If these high stakes are not handled properly, your company, customers, and employees may have to pay the price.

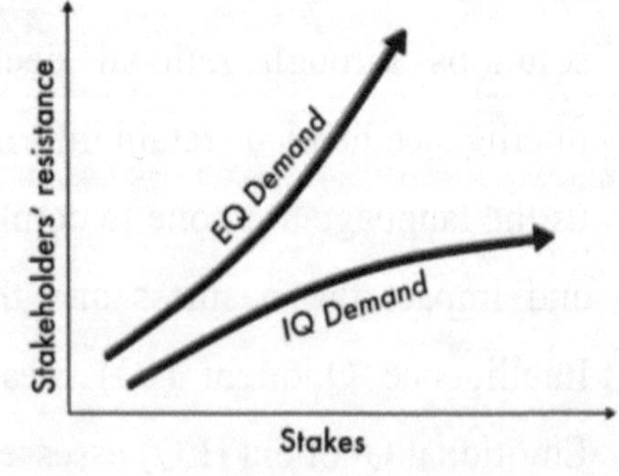

Stakes & EQ Chart

If the ability to understand and use emotions can be considered a form of intelligence, group Emotional Intelligence is even more important since most of the work in business is executed in a team environment. A group EQ score isn't simply the sum of individuals' EQ scores in that group. Rather, it's the ability of the group to effectively communicate on an emotional level as a single unit. It is humanly impossible to assume that every team member is on the same emotional wavelength. Therefore, it is important that we understand and respect each other's emotions.

Agile Methodology is Effective, How About Some Emotional Agility?

The term "Agile Methodology" was introduced in the IT industry in the year 2000, and yet it didn't become popular across the board until the last few years. *Agile is a mindset, not just a methodology – as an agile transformation coach once told me.* Emotionally agile leaders are capable of handling unexpected and adverse situations and adapting to changes efficiently. Are you and your team emotionally agile? Can you adapt and respond effectively to your changing environment while also being aware of your thoughts, emotions, behavior, and actions?

An effective and deliberate leader doesn't try to suppress a group member's thoughts, feelings, and emotions. Instead, they approach each person in a mindful, value-driven, and productive way using emotional agility.

It's not possible to be free of emotions, nor should it be expected that everyone on your team is at the same emotional level. But becoming more emotionally agile will make you an effective leader, while remaining emotionally rigid will only hinder you. You can be emotionally intelligent but still lack emotional agility.

For example, among many other practical techniques, this book discusses a process called the "labeling technique," a way to handle a complex situation in a graceful, agile, and non-judgmental way. The first step is to notice when your behavior is driven by rigid and repetitive thoughts and habits. You need not block out difficult emotions; just be mindful of your feeling and experience. As a high-EQ leader, you'll notice as you unhook yourself from your negative emotions and start to expand the "menu" of reactions to difficult situations. Then you can act, so it aligns with your and your organization's core values. In the audio version of this book, I have provided a step-by-step technique you can follow to improve your emotional agility.

Becoming agile with your emotions can then help you foster this skill in your team. To create high group EQ, it might be necessary to offer your team a safe environment to share their thoughts and feelings. This will foster trust and collaboration and will help improve employee engagement. They will develop a capacity to face adverse situations collectively. Such emotional connection goes a long way, as it affects not just employees but also the company's internal and external stakeholders.

Information sharing, cross-functional collaboration, and healthy risk-taking are essential in today's businesses. Being agile by facilitating cross-cultural communication and understanding the nuances of different people can be a true competitive advantage. A deliberate leader with sound Emotional Intelligence creates an environment of trust and cooperation across the board.

Relevance of Emotional Intelligence in Decision Making

Leaders know their actions have consequences. They also understand they have to earn positive results one decision at a time. Consistently making the right decisions takes problem-solving and emotional control. But how do you know what the "right" decisions are? In business, there are always more gray areas than black and white. F. Scott Fitzgerald once famously wrote - "The test of a first-rate intelligence is the ability to hold two opposing ideas in mind at the same time and still retain the ability to function." In business, if you are trying to make a decision for absolute right versus absolute wrong, that doesn't challenge your intelligence as much. If your decision evaluates both sides of perspectives, you will better utilize your intelligence and make more sound decisions.

Now, think about how you make decisions. You don't necessarily stop and make a conscious decision to engage your Emotional Intelligence. Instead, you make decisions primarily through an unconscious process that neuroscientists call pattern recognition and emotional tagging. What this means in practical terms is you make quick decisions by recognizing patterns in the situations you encounter. Deliberate leaders can make quick and effective decisions without thinking. In effect, the best leaders have internalized the habits of emotionally intelligent leadership, and when they act, they do so without a script or a manual.

However, decision-making can often be distorted by self-interest and misleading memories. Leaders need to recognize the source of bias called "red flag condition" and design safeguards to avoid biased decision-making, thus avoiding flawed decisions.

This is not to say that conscious decision-making is not important. On the contrary, decisions must be made using reason and active, conscious decision-making. Cognitive Intelligence (rational, conscious intelligence) and Emotional Intelligence have different profiles, and they often go hand in hand. I'm not advocating one over the other. In fact, I argue that deliberate leaders possess both traits in abundance, and they integrate them into their workplace.

Anytime you are in a dilemma about the decision you are going to make, pause for a moment, step back and think - what are your leadership values? They might be described as dependability, diligence, tolerance, authority, autonomy, flexibility, rationality, stability, moderation, or mindfulness. Once you've identified your values, you can use this knowledge to help you navigate a challenging situation at work. Next time you make a difficult decision, stop and ask yourself whether your actions align with your stated values.

Emotional Intelligence cannot exist in a vacuum. By itself, Emotional Intelligence or any leadership principle is not a cure-all that will immediately improve a business's performance. Emotional Intelligence must be coupled with technical literacy in one's field. It must be tethered to one's problem-solving abilities, relevant experience, and digital literacy. When these elements are combined, there is no limit to what a business can achieve.

The emotional and deliberate leadership approach described in this book hinges on four principles in today's day and age:

Developing Emotional Competency Relationship building and influencing mindsets	**Promoting Positive Emotional Contagion** Driving group performance and strategic sales
Leading with Emotional Agility Tactical empathy and mind-body intelligence	**Building Emotional Resiliency** Leading through changes, crisis, and M&A

I know you are a busy leader or executive, and time is of the essence. With that in mind, I wrote this book in such a way you don't need to read it in the order it was written. Feel free to flip to a page at random and see what you find. Or, if you are focusing on an area or situation of your business, head over to that chapter. *If your company or group is going through changes (or resisting changes), go straight to Chapter 8, "Leading Changes with Emotional Intelligence." Likewise, if you need to revisit your salesforce strategy, go to Chapter 5, "Emotional Intelligence in Strategic Sales." If your company or group is going through a merger or acquisition or recently had one, visit Chapter 9, "Managing Emotions in Mergers & Acquisitions." If you want to learn about what science has revealed how you can improve your cognitive and emotional health, read Chapter 10,*

"Leading with Mind, Body & Soul." And so on.

I wrote this book to empower leaders like you to motivate their employees, create value for stakeholders, and take your business to the next level. Based on my own experience and that of the experts and researchers I've interviewed, I wholeheartedly believe that the principles described within are some of the most effective tools for addressing technological and social change in the workplace.

Look at your organization. You'll find that at its heart lies in process and values. The human element is the common link between these two. Look closer, and you'll realize that the same emotions summoned to increase a company's productivity are often the same forces that can undermine a company's core values. Many organizations still function in an outdated way, refusing to examine the processes and values that drive their business. The principles, tools, and techniques described in this book can help you unlock the full potential of your leadership abilities. The forthcoming chapters will guide you to become a more mindful leader, which means you will develop a moment-by-moment awareness of your emotions in a wide range of business situations and environments. So please join me on this journey as we take these intelligent and deliberate leadership lessons and apply them to the most pressing decisions we as leaders face today.

Chapter 2

Influencing Mindset—with or without Authority

"All that we are is the result of what we have thought. The mind is everything. What we think, we shall become."

—Buddha, 623 B.C.

Not just people, even animals grapple to establish a hierarchy in their kingdom. Animals assert their dominance in ways such as eye contact, body language, and growling. Sometimes we do too. But most of the time, people show their dominance ranging from subtle gestures to show their authority and positional power to influence people. In this chapter, you will learn how to use the principles of emotional intelligence and deliberate leadership to influence mindset - with or without positional power.

A mindset influences how people think, feel, and behave in any situation. The question is, when the business requires, how can you influence mindset for the greater good. Whether you are an individual contributor, manager, or executive, much of your business success depends on how you influence others' mindsets and how you reflect your mindset (your projection).

Influencing is about understanding what others tick and knowing how to effectively communicate with them to help them reach their and your goal. When you introduce a new concept or a change, do not try to change people's minds or *mindsets*. Instead, focus on getting them to change their *behavior*. This will have a two-fold effect - they will get to see your point of view firsthand, and they'd can do a better job or aim for a better goal.

The better we understand what others think and feel, the more we'll be able to influence them. This is where you'll see your emotional intelligence in play. We can't read people's minds. But we can observe, listen and ask relevant questions to understand their viewpoint. This way, we can engage in meaningful conversations that generate a sense of ownership in others. There are as many ways to influence as there are kinds of people in the world. Different people respond to different styles of influence and types of communication. Some people you work with may be technical, others analytical, and others are more business oriented. The tools you can use to influence can be logical or emotional, depending on the people you are trying to influence. Understanding which technique to use will help you influence various types of mindsets in different situations. After you discover which influencing tools to use, you will start to influence them in the right direction and see their mindset reorienting.

Influencing the behavior of your coworkers and team members is vitally important if your business or organization is going to maximize its potential. But don't forget, what takes place in the workplace is just one piece of the puzzle. Influencing the mindset of people beyond your office—including your customers—can also help you achieve your goals.

Leading companies know how to influence the public's mindset through marketing and branding. After all, getting your customer base to think highly of your product or brand is just another way of saying that you're influencing their mindset.

Good companies influence "minds" using their brand, but great and revolutionary companies influence "mindset," and they become the industry leader. Consider Japanese entrepreneur Satoshi Nakamoto. He created the first cryptocurrency in 2009 following the housing market crash. This was the first product in an entirely new industry. After that, over 4,000 cryptocurrencies came into existence (with more added by the day).

Or consider 5G mobile networks. The telecommunications providers at the cutting edge of 5G are setting the wireless standard for the entire industry. Airbnb and Uber influenced their customers using a new concept, the "share economy," which created a new business model. You see, when it comes to great companies and great leaders, customers don't really care about the brands. They care about concepts (or categories) that influence mindset.

Influence with Direct Authority

Often (but not always), authority can be a good and readily available tool to develop your leadership influence. Because of your track record, influence, decisiveness, and inspiration, you can help your team accomplish your collective goals. As a leader, you may have power, but try to hold it in reserve and rely on authority to lead.

As a business leader or manager, you are passionate about your company's projects you are spearheading. You know that what you're working on, or what you're proposing, will make a radical shift in the paradigm and how your company does business. But does your team share that level of passion? When you positively influence the mindset of people you manage, you can see how their efforts ignite their innate abilities and turn your initiatives into concrete accomplishments for the common good of your business or organization. When you're positively influencing them, they will talk about the project and execute it with the same level of passion and fun you have, and they get thrilled just talking about it. That's when you know you are changing their mindset.

At an organizational level, talent is passed down in mindset. A progressive and persuasive mindset builds the character of your team members and your entire business. This character, combined with resilience and applied toward long-term goals, makes an individual, group, or organization gritty.

In today's workplace, employee performance follows the Pareto Principle (the 80/20 rule) – 20 percent of employees shoulder 80 percent of the responsibility and work. Look around you. It's no doubt that 20 percent are high achievers who have extraordinary stamina. Even if they're already at the top of their projects, they're continually trying to improve the process or techniques they employ. They don't try to take shortcuts; they like to get to the root of problems and tackle fundamental challenges. This combination of strengths and skills is what makes "grit."

Most of your business is taken care of by a small minority of such gritty employees. They're the floor leaders, the ones who know what to do and often just take care of things without your asking. They're the project leaders who take the ball and run with it, who give 125 percent because they exemplify personal excellence. Sometimes, these people will be prominent and easy to identify; other times, it may be harder to figure out who they are. As a leader, you'll want to figure out who these people are. Appreciate them and reward them occasionally. They may be real role models, and they may even be future leaders in your organization.

Now, imagine you have an employee who has this mindset. How do you channel their perspective and influence them in the right direction to meet your organization's needs? It's not always easy and not always instantaneous, but if you take the time to influence your top-performing employees, the results can be astonishing.

Let's look at four ways to influence that outstanding team member and future leader. How can you influence that person to take their work to the next level, and how can you focus their energy to help your business?

1. Be a role model
2. Demonstrate conviction
3. Show care to influence your vision
4. Use performance appraisals to influence behavior

1. Be a role model

Modeling the behavior, you would like to see your employees emulate is a subtly powerful way to influence them. Think back to when you were looking to your leaders for guidance in the workplace. You probably looked to successful managers and leaders, and you tried to follow their lead and do as they did. Maybe they were fantastic communicators. Perhaps they worked harder or smarter than anyone else. Maybe they commanded the respect of their co-workers because they were models of integrity or intelligence. For whatever reason, you looked up to them and learned from them.

Don't expect to be always loved and be appreciated for your views by those who work for you. You will be up against many of the ideas and changes you're introducing. When you're being a role model, don't be so subtle that your behavior goes unnoticed. Be deliberate about it. You want to make sure your team members notice what you're doing so they can follow your lead. If you want to inspire teamwork, for example, go out of your way to embody the traits you desire—roll up your sleeves and work with others on a project so they can see how it's done. That's what a good role model does. And that's what you can do to influence the people working for you.

2. Demonstrate conviction

This is a more direct way to influence your team. Rather than modeling behavior—*doing* this involves explaining your vision and convincing them why they should buy into it. First, you need them to understand your vision, and that requires *clarity*. If your vision is for the whole organization to work together to increase sales by 10 percent, be clear this is your goal.

Next, you need them to believe in your vision, and that requires *conviction*. Clarity without conviction won't influence people to buy into your vision. You need to explain why your plan is a good one. Increasing sales by 10 percent is one thing, but it's unlikely to inspire them to work harder. You might explain that your goal is for the entire team to pull together to accomplish a difficult task that will make the company an industry leader.

3. Show care to influence your vision

If your employees know you care about their future, you are more likely to influence them to carry out your vision. Communicating how their work will teach them new skills and improve their performance is an excellent way to inspire them.

Explaining how you're investing in the growth of your team members will inspire them to invest in the growth of your business or organization. Be clear about how the skills they will gain working on a specific project could be applied to future work. You might even tell them how far they've come along and how impressed you are with their progress in the workplace.

4. Use performance appraisals to influence behavior

Compared to being a role model, this is on the other end of the spectrum. It is overt and to the point and involves giving your employees direct feedback about their work. This method could come in the form of periodic reviews or informal, continuous appraisals. In either case, you tell your team member how they are doing and how they can improve. If you want them to improve their strategic thinking, you can focus on this problem in a discussion detailing ways they can improve.

Also tell them why they should make the behavioral change you want to see. If you want them to focus on bringing in new clients, for example, you could explain how this personal goal dovetails with the purposes of the entire organization.

You can also influence them by detailing the consequences of making the behavior change. This could be a positive incentive, such as a bonus or the opportunity for advancement within the organization, or it could be a negative incentive. However, use negative incentives only as a last resort because you'll see much better results by influencing them using positive mechanisms.

Influencing Mindset Without Positional Power

This is more challenging and rewarding than the previous influencing techniques presented that uses "authority" or "positional power" to an extent. With positional power, your influence is mainly limited to your team buy the techniques described in this section can be used to influence other groups, external stakeholders, prospects, and customers.

You might find yourself occasionally in a position without the power to influence others. But a true leader doesn't need positional power to inspire mindsets. **It's easy to confuse *control*, which comes from positional power, and *influence*, which depends on your actions no matter where you fall in the company hierarchy.**

If you don't have positional power, you can still influence or inspire others. No matter what your position is, you have many tools at your disposal. I have listed ten techniques you can use to influence mindsets without positional power or authority.

Change your perspective.

You can't influence someone else's mindset unless you are willing to change your own. Changing your thoughts and feelings translates into changes in behavior. Businesses will have ups and downs, and there may be low points in your interactions with coworkers. Suppose you had a negative interaction with one of your stakeholders (or prospects), and you have an upcoming meeting to convince them about a proposed project. In that case, it's best first to change your perspective about them. Stay calm, be consistent in your behavior, and treat the next interaction as a chance to wipe the slate clean.

Treat people as allies.

In the workplace, we all need each other. It can sometimes seem like it's "everyone for themselves", but we're all working toward the same goal at the end of the day. You need to create trust in work environment. Treating people as allies means you respect and believe in them and trust their vision. Treat people as allies, and they will return the favor.

Don't make it personal.

You can influence people's behavior, but there are limits—you can't control what they do. Remember that how people react is because of them, not because of you. If someone you work with is sullen, dismissive, or unconvinced about your ideas, that doesn't mean they don't like you as a person. They might even be right—maybe your idea could use some revamping. Treat these negative interactions as learning opportunities. Above all, don't overreact and respond with negative energy. When you react with understanding, this is a form of nonverbal communication that will promote belief in your leadership abilities.

Give people the benefit of the doubt.

See the best in your coworkers, and assume they have good intentions. Everyone has bad days, and if someone on your team is less than kind to you, consider they may have their own problems they're working through. This positive mindset will allow you to make new allies. Similarly, if a teammate or coworker is not doing the work you think they're capable of, consider that although they may be trying, organizational structures aren't up to bringing out the best in them. They might rise to the occasion and be an all-star contributor if they receive the right positive influences down the line.

Treat people like you want to be treated.

Even better, try to treat them as *they* wish to be treated. In life and business, it's always best to be decent and treat people with dignity and respect. As I discussed in chapter 6 on *Empathy as a Competitive Advantage in the Business*, it is in your power to be genuine and sincere in how you react and what you do.

Influence thoughts to influence behavior and mindset.

If you want a specific behavioral outcome—whether it's increased effort or to make a sale—start by influencing the thoughts of the person you're talking with. This begins with asking the right questions that will make them think. These are proven strategies also in simple to complex selling. **If you make a statement, they listen to them "passively," but if you ask them questions, it will compel them to think more "actively."** Thoughts follow actions.

I have used the strategy of questioning in team environments a lot. When I worked at Microsoft, I saw many engineers were working in silos. Many individual contributors didn't realize someone else in another group on the same floor had solved that problem. When someone came with a new problem, I would ask them three whys. The "3 Whys Technique" is precisely what you think it is: asking the question "why?" three times to get to the real root of a question or problem. This questioning often brought forth a solution, and we would find that the problem had been solved by someone else. That solution could then be applied to the new situation, leading to teammates communicating and collaborating instead of reinventing wheels.

By no means am I attempting to provide you with cookie-cutter tactics, but I hope this will show you how to navigate a variety of workplace situations.

Before presenting a new idea, talk to difficult stakeholders.

Remember, you're not in this alone. By taking the time to speak with the stakeholders you'll be submitting a project or proposal to, you can ask them for their input. A simple question like, "I'm curious what you thought of my proposal" will invite them to be active participants in your presentation. That will make them co-owners of the problem. They will want to help you solve it — and they will become your ally.

Answer the "What's in it for me?" question.

This is usually an unspoken question, but if you can explain to the person how following your lead will benefit them, they'll be much more likely to support your vision. When the result of an action is in a person's best interest, they are more likely to do it. That's not to say that people are inherently selfish but telling them how it affects them can be an additional motivating factor in getting them to act.

Establish a fact-based culture for influencing.

There is a key difference between offering facts and offering opinions. And when influencing mindset, it is essential to state reality rather than your own read on a situation. For example, if you want a coworker to contribute more, it is more effective to say, "I finished five projects this month, and I noticed you completed two" than it is to say, "I think I might have done more work than you this month." Bringing facts to bear on a situation is always more powerful.

Consider timing.

In business, as in life, timing is everything. Know when it's an opportune time to make your case and promote your vision and know when it's best to step back and bide your time. If the whole organization is under the stress of a deadline, it will be better to wait until you have their full attention.

Promoting Growth Mindset in your Organization

Ultimately, your goal should be to inspire your team to feel great about the work they do so they can grow. To do this, creating an atmosphere of trust is far more effective than an atmosphere of judgment.

In the words of psychologist Carol Dweck, "When bosses become controlling and abusive, they put everyone into a fixed mindset. This means that instead of learning, growing, and moving the company forward, everyone starts worrying about being judged. It starts with the bosses' worry about being judged, but it winds up being everybody's fear about being judged. It's hard for courage and innovation to survive in a company-wide fixed mindset."

To start with, you have to make sure that *you* have a growth mindset about your organization. If you think, "The people working for me have limits, and that limits what we can achieve as a business," then you're in a fixed mindset. Being a leader is about being open, flexible, and believing that your team can achieve greatness.

When you have a growth mindset, that positivity is infectious. People who work for you might have a fixed mindset and not believe in their own potential for growth, but if you believe in them—and if you communicate that belief—they will start to believe in themselves. That's the magic of a growth mindset.

Fear of failure is one of the biggest impediments to a growth mindset. If people in your organization think they'll be judged, belittled, or punished for failing, they will feel stuck in a fixed mindset. Show them that failure is necessary on the path to success by taking risks and not being afraid to be wrong once in a while. Admit when you're wrong, and be persistent in tackling challenges, and your employees will follow.

Perseverance and resilience are outcomes of a growth mindset, and this is what you should foster in your team. Praise them for their effort, focus, process, strategy, motivation, belief, and emotions—not just their talent, ability, and outcomes. Assessment of the performance alone is incomplete. Focus on the process, not just the outcome. In the growth mindset, the meaning of failure changes to "lessons learned." If you do this, your team will be willing to seek more challenges.

In any team, you will encounter individuals who look for constant validation. Rather than seeing this as a hindrance to the team's work, take the time to groom these employees, increase their confidence, and provide them with constructive criticism. Remember, everyone is capable of growth.

Just because some people can execute a project with hardly any training doesn't mean others can't execute it with a little help. If you don't create a supportive atmosphere, you'll have a lot of wasted talent on your team. Think about those employees who need encouragement as untapped potential in your company and group. If you create a "help me help you" atmosphere, it will allow your group to utilize team members' full potential.

Sometimes, our actions can communicate that we undervalue employees who need additional help to succeed. That's why team bonuses can help encourage an "all hands-on deck" mentality and demonstrate to the team that everyone is valuable—not just the highest-performing members. In a 2014 survey of 350 publicly traded U.S. companies, only 28 percent said they use team incentives. Most of the companies I have worked with had group and individual-based performance incentives, and I have witnessed the power of rewarding the whole team.

In every organization, hiring managers want to hire the best and brightest for the job, but it doesn't always happen. Many companies believe in "natural talents," but ironically, they often show rigidness and arrogance in identifying talent. Furthermore, it's not necessarily the case that the most suitable candidate is ready to accept the offer for your group at that time and is willing to relocate to the geographic area where you need the hire. That's why you need to focus on continuous grooming and training of employees, managers, and leaders. In other words, focus on encouraging a growth mindset among all your employees, even those who haven't been identified as "natural talents."

Fixed mindset and growth mindset are not fixed states of mind. With exemplary leadership and tools, anyone with the right attitude can do well and create value in your team.

Understanding human behavior and influencing tools

As I mentioned earlier, even animals use eye contact, body language, and sound to show their stand. Sometimes we do too. You need to understand the three elements of human communication. Words, body language, and tone constitute the basic tools you have when you want to be influence someone. Because all three work together, it's worth taking a deep look at each.

Influencing Mindset with Body Language and Tone

Regardless of the influencing methods you use, what you say and how you say it is important. We need to understand the nature of communication in behavior.

Only a tiny fraction of our communication is verbal. The graphic below shows that only 7 percent of communication comes from words, while the overwhelming majority comes from nonverbal cues: 38 percent through tone and 55 percent through body language[1].

7 - 38 - 55% Communication Rule

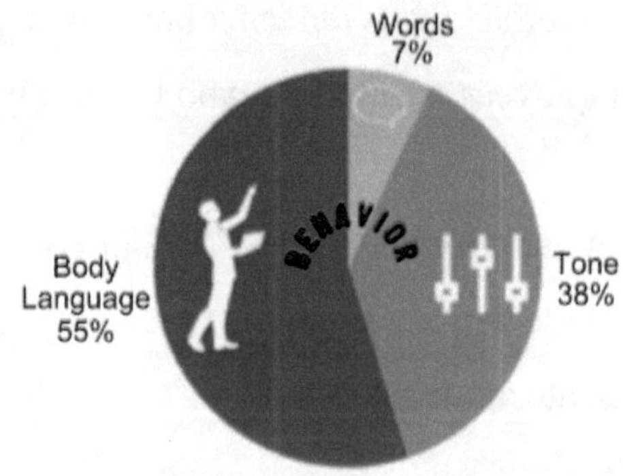

Body language includes everything from your posture and hand movements to your smile and eye contact. Building trust can be accomplished—or undermined by body language and facial expressions that either support or undercut what you're saying. For example, if you say, "Nice to meet you," but you're grimacing and forget to shake the person's hand, your body and face are

---

[1] In 1960s Albert Mehrabian developed the 7-38-55% rule.

communicating that you're not all that enthusiastic about the interaction. That's why it's extremely important to be aware of the nonverbal ways that you're communicating.

The idea that first impressions are important is a commonly held belief for a good reason. When you meet someone, they tend to form an impression of you within the first seven seconds. The basis of their first impression is largely determined by nonverbal cues such as body language and facial expressions.

When you're trying to communicate your leadership, your body speaks louder than words. So even if the words you're using are confident, if your face is communicating uncertainty or worry, you will give an overall impression of timidity. To communicate that you are trustworthy and open, all the kind words in the world won't leave that impression if your arms are crossed and your demeanor communicates that you're closed off and defensive. As a leader, you need to convey confidence through your body language. Stand straight and tall, with an open posture and a relaxed facial expression.

Your tone is the second most important element of leaving your team with a positive impression. Just as with body language, how you say something is often more important than what you say. In fact, the tone of your voice can undermine your message if you aren't conscious of how you're speaking. The good news is that you can control your tone. Elements like volume (loud or soft), pitch (high or low), and speed (quickly or slowly) are within your control. In projecting leadership qualities, you want to aim for a relaxed delivery, which means slowing down, speaking up, and not raising the pitch of your voice. Scientists who have studied the communication of successful business leaders have shown these elements can increase a leader's charisma, which can ultimately help you be a better influencer.

Words if chosen deliberately, can be leveraged to influence. However, the choice of words has only a 7% contribution in influencing. You may wonder why, if the choice of words has such a negligible effect on business communication, there is so much emphasis on speech in business education. That is because language has specifically intended emotional effects that can evoke an emotional response in the listener or reader. Words aren't the whole story, but they are important. There are "positive hot button" words for each person. If you use those words, you don't have to repeat the instruction or proposal over and over again. On the other hand, there are "negative hot button" words for each person. If you use those words, no matter how much you try, the person will not like your proposal, or you will have to work way too hard to convince them. For example, consider the words "goal" and "task." For a member of your team who is driven to succeed, you could describe a project you're assigning them as a "task." But this could be a negative hot button word for them, as it communicates drudgery and dullness. "Goal," on the other hand, is a positive hot-button word because it connotes challenge, growth, and purpose.

How can you know the most effective way to communicate with your team? The Whole Brain® Thinking theory, developed by Ned Herrmann, offers some helpful guidance. This system divides brain into four quadrants and provides examples of how different kinds of words can influence people with different mindsets. They can be your employees, stakeholders, partners, prospects, or customers.

Let's consider the best language to use for each profile.[2]

Personality Types

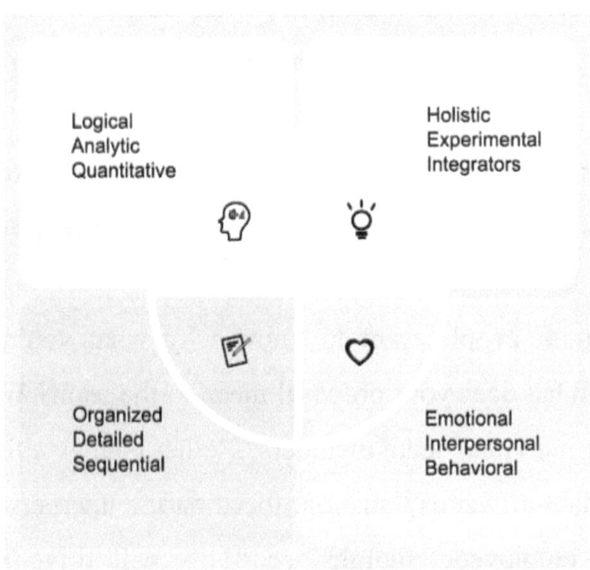

Logical people respond to hard data. Use numbers, track records, forecasts to get your point across. Analytical people do not take anything for granted, so be specific. Instead of describing the goals of a proposal vaguely, say — "This proposal is designed to reduce

---

[2] Developed by Ned Herrmann, Whole Brain® Thinking divides the brain into these four quadrants. In his actual explanation, quadrant "A" include - Logical, Analytic, Fact based & Quantitative. Quadrant "B" has - Organized, Sequential, Planned & Detailed. Quadrant "C" covers Interpersonal, Feeling based, Kinesthetic & Emotional. Lastly, quadrant "D" shows - holistic, intuitive integrating and Synthesizing.

customer churn by 4% annually." Also, if you have customers in this profile, you may have to prove yourself constantly. Build rapport again and again by pointing to your track record of delivering for them and exceeding their expectations.

Organized people want to hear the complete plan before acting. Provide them with the specifics of your proposal, followed by your opinion. Explain to them what is important before showing them the solution. If you are writing them an email, don't skimp on the details. Provide an explanation of why you're asking them to do something, stating what you want them to do. If you send them a short email on the discussion topic, they may think you have oversimplified the message.

Emotional people want to know why what you're doing is important. What does your proposal mean to the team? What does it mean to the individual team members? Rather than give them a nuts-and-bolts, data-driven explanation, focus on the interpersonal. "This will boost employees' morale" or "This will drive away your customers' dissatisfaction" is a better way to influence them than describing the plan in too much detail.

Holistic people also like minimal details, but they still want to explore different ideas and options simultaneously. They excel at drawing conclusions and integrating information, so provide them with the big picture. Use short and caption-like words, along with visuals and charts to explain. For example, you could show a chart of declining survey responses and explain the need to change the campaign content.

If you aren't sure which profile fits an employee, pay attention to their own communication style and choice of words, and that will help you figure out what group they are in. And then you can match their style when you speak with them.

Some people may be a combination of profiles depending on the situation. Outside of work, they may be holistic and outgoing, but they may be more emotional or sensitive at work. If you sense this behavior in a person working for you, it can be helpful to use softer language to avoid intimidating them, such as these phrases:

"I trust your instincts, but most people go for this option."

"It's up to you."

"I'll leave it up to you to decide."

"I wanted to run something by you to get your input."

"Let's try to work this out together."

You can also rephrase directives as questions:

"Have you considered…?"

"What if you were to make this change?"

"Would you like to see some examples?"

This is also a good strategy for communicating with people outside of your organization, such as customers or prospects. Instead of your customer support team saying, "I can't handle this question, I need to connect you with a higher tier rep," they can say, "Would you mind if I escalated this to a higher tier support team member to see if they can identify what the issue might be here?"

Another effective practice for communicating with external sources is to follow the lead of their communication style. For example, when you submit a bid, respond to them in the same language and style as the bid requests. For government bids, especially, follow the style more closely.

No matter the profile of the person you're working with, don't leave them in a negative state of mind, regardless of conversation. When you end a conversation with anyone, end with a word of encouragement. That's what will linger in their mind and stay with them emotionally after they leave the discussion. You will realize giving sincere and relevant compliments is the most powerful tactic in business. When you do so, you will feel the surge of your own influence on others. Also, people love to be around positive people and will be more likely to follow your example and listen to your ideas.

The Role of Empathy in Influencing Mindset

How can you influence someone if you don't know what they're thinking? Unless you can "see" their world from their shoes, you won't be able to maximize your influence. When people feel heard and understood, they are more likely to respond positively to your influence. That's where empathy comes into play. Refer to the chapter "*Empathy - Competitive Advantage in Business*" in this book.

Empathy boils down to being cognizant of how other people are feeling. To practice empathy, start by listening. You can't know what the other person is going through if you don't ask questions. Hear everything they want to say before you jump in and respond. After they have finished speaking, thank them for sharing their thoughts. It's also a great idea to reiterate areas of shared experience and interest. For example, if your coworker divulges that they are experiencing difficulty managing their work-life balance, you could respond by saying, "I understand what you're going through. I also find it tough to balance my family responsibilities and my workload." This is using empathy to forge a meaningful connection.

Harvard Law Professor Robert Mnookin says that empathy is different than just being nice or agreeing with another person. In fact, you don't necessarily have to have shared experiences to forge a connection. Even if you disagree with someone, you can employ "tactical empathy" to ensure that they feel understood. Instead of openly disagreeing with someone, you can say, "I hear you, and I understand your concerns," before moving on to a solution.

The difference between influencing minds and influencing mindset is the difference between increasing the size of the slice and increasing the slice of the pie. Think about that next time you're considering the importance of influencing mindset.

Mindset, as we have seen, is everything in the business world. With the right mindset, average employees can become exceptional, and merely effective leaders can become role models. The entire nature of an organization can change when leaders influence their team for the good of the company.

Fortunately, influencing mindset within your company is well within your reach. As we have seen, tools like body language, tone, and word choice have a vast impact when you're trying to motivate people. As you grow as a leader and help your company grow use these tips to generate an organizational feeling of purpose and excellence. Mindset determines not only the financial success of your company. It also affects the lives at work and beyond—of the people on your team. And remember, you don't need to wait to gain authority to be a leader at your company. As Ken Blanchard said – *"The key to successful leadership is influence, not authority"*.

Chapter 3

Flow State Leadership and Igniting Motivation

"Flow is being completely involved in an activity for its own sake. The ego falls away. Time flies. Every action, movement, and thought follows inevitably from the previous one, like playing jazz."

—Mihaly Csikszentmihalyi

Picture yourself in the office on a Tuesday afternoon. You've just gotten back from lunch, and you have what seems like a million tasks on your to-do list. You're not even sure where to begin. Frankly, this mountain of work feels intimidating and slightly overwhelming. You ask yourself, "How on earth am I going to get this done?"

So, what do you do? You jump right in without a second thought. You put on your headphones, put some classical music on, and start in on item number one. Within fifteen minutes, you're in a groove. The work that seemed so daunting just minutes ago now seems completely manageable. Task one is completed, and you're in a groove, so you move on to number two. Then number three and number four.

By the time you're checking the last item off your to-do list, you glance at the clock for the first time all afternoon. "How is it 6:30 p.m. already?" you think.

We've all had experiences like this—and we all cherish those days when the work comes easy. The days when you're in a groove, the days when you're "in a flow."

But what is "flow"? As it turns out, there is a good deal of scientific research on this mind-state.

In 1990, Hungarian-American psychologist Mihaly Csikszentmihalyi was the first to identify and research "Flow." In Mihaly's words, Flow (the psychology of optimal experience) is "*a state in which people are so involved in an activity that nothing else seems to matter; the experience is so enjoyable that people will continue to do it even at great cost, for the sheer sake of doing it.*" In simple words - the sense of time and ego goes away in the "flow" state. The only thing that matters is the task at hand. The big question that managers and employees alike want to answer is: how can you access this state of pleasant productivity in the workplace and manage your team's energy?

It's hard enough to access a state of flow whenever you need it. It's even harder to create a group flow state that will allow all of your employees to fire on all cylinders. Whether you're responsible for project management process, production lines, or sales systems, you need to manage the energy in your group. After all, your business is an orchestra, not a solo performance. Your employee needs to work together to make your business run. Just as an orchestra depends on the virtuosity of individual players, you need your employees to give their best. But you also need them to play together as they hear one another's music notes in real-time.

Business is an Orchestra

In Mihaly's words, *"flow is an addiction."* That feeling of complete confidence and ease that comes with the flow state is something that each of us wants to return to again and again. And as a business owner or manager, what you want to do is create the conditions that can allow your employees to get in a state of flow—both individually and as a group. In group flow, people feel self-suspended and self-extended. They're excelling at their work, and they feel empowered and motivated to help their co-workers. Performance becomes contagious, and the team creates a sense of purpose. The group stops being a collection of individuals and becomes a "common self" with a motivation that transcends the work of individuals. This creates meaning, purpose, and happiness. And the good news is, you as a leader, there is much you can do to promote this level of team engagement.

Promoting Flow in the Workplace

Now that we know what flow is and why it's desirable for your company let's look at how you can help your employees achieve this level of momentum. When we talk about flow, we're talking about dopamine. Dopamine is a neurotransmitter that scientists believe plays a key role in the experience of pleasure. When you see your children or when your dog greets you when you come home, you're getting a hit of dopamine. When you bite into a juicy steak or take a sip of nice red wine, your brain is producing dopamine. And when you're working on a project and excelling at your work—you guessed it, you're feeling the dopamine your brain produced. Dopamine does more than provide pleasure, though. It also provides us with a sense of focus and drive, which in turn can get us into a state of flow.

What do you suppose is the most common way employees in an office increase their dopamine levels? If you said "coffee," you're right. That's because caffeine enhances dopamine signaling in the brain. There's a reason caffeine is the most widely consumed psychoactive substance in the world. And there's a reason it's so well-adapted for the work environment. We use it not just because it makes us feel good—though of course, it does—but also to promote wakefulness and enhance alertness. As we all know, the problem with caffeine is those feelings of wakefulness and alertness are short-lived. We all know what it feels like to have that "coffee crash" at 11 am. That is because, in the average body, the caffeine in a cup of coffee doesn't last over two hours. Now, one way to solve the coffee crash problem is to switch to tea. And that's what many of us drink. Plenty of people don't prefer coffee's taste. Many others might be sick of the coffee crash, and they want a longer-lasting dopamine rush. Tea, it turns out, can be a good substitute for coffee, and its effect lasts longer. Even tea, though, tends to wear off after about four hours. Like coffee, the effects of tea are short-lived. No matter what amount of caffeine one has, the average focus span is less than twenty minutes. After that, the average human brain either starts to wander or begins to seek distractions.

Don't you and your team want to feel alert, awake, and pleasant for longer than a couple of hours? Wouldn't it be better if we were operating at our maximum efficiency for the entire duration of the day? Of course, it would. So maybe the problem isn't the type of caffeine we consume. Perhaps we need something else—we need to be in a state of flow more often.

Ways to Maximize Flow at Work

This leads us back to the key question: how can you foster a work environment that promotes flow? Steven Kotler, the founder of the Flow Genome Project, has studied flow in the workplace extensively. He recommends several "triggers" that can get individuals—and groups—in a state of flow. According to Kotler's research, you can promote individual flow by implementing these changes in your workplace:

Provide timely—or, better yet, immediate—feedback.

If you want your employees to stay focused and confident, there's no better way than to tell them they're doing a great job (or tell them what they can improve). This instantaneous feedback will allow them to adjust their performance in real-time.

Layout clear, tangible goals.

One of the best ways to promote individual flow is to be clear about the goals you want your employees to meet. Break up complex, multi-step tasks into a series of smaller, discrete steps. Make these goals tangible, too. Instead of providing vague benchmarks ("You're doing good, but I want you to do *great*"), tell your employees exactly how they can improve ("I want you to decrease your errors by 10%").

Offer reasonable challenges.

You don't want your employees to get bored or feel that their complete skill set is being underutilized. If that happens, they'll find it hard to get in a flow state. Setting up solvable challenges for your employees is critical because you want them to feel engaged.

Eliminate distractions.

If you want your employees to stay focused and inflow, the good news is that as their boss, you can do your part by eliminating distractions. Don't be afraid to encourage solo time. That also means being conscientious about emails and meetings. You might even set up company-wide days when email and meetings are discouraged. If that's not realistic, let your employees know that you don't expect them to read or respond to email immediately.

Have fun.

There's a difference between an office focused and occasionally quiet and one that feels more like a library. Introduce a bit of fun and novelty to your workplace. There's a reason so many Silicon Valley companies (and many others) have foosball tables and scooters on their campuses: it encourages employees to let their spirit of play come out. And with that sense of freedom will come an increased chance of flow.

By implementing these changes in your office or business, you can encourage individual and group flow. In doing so, you will create a workplace that employees enjoy being a part of. What's more, you will see the productivity and innovation of your employee's soar.

As we've seen, it's important to create a work environment that promotes flow in individual employees. But even better is to foster the conditions for group flow. Kotler's research suggests you can encourage flow group by doing the following:

Communicate clearly.

Without a good conductor, even a roomful of experienced, skilled musicians can't play a Beethoven symphony. Similarly, even an office full of talented, motivated employees can't work together to their full effectiveness without a clear communicator at the top. So, communicate clearly and openly with your whole team.

Create common goals.

If you want everyone in your workplace to come together for the greater good of the business, you need to do more than set benchmarks for individual employees. Make goals that the entire team can work toward together, independent of their individual contributions. That way, your employees in a flow state can help when their co-workers are struggling.

Get everyone on the same page.

You can't have group flow if you're not engaging meaningfully with all of your employees. You can eliminate "silos" and cliques by looping everyone in on important communications, regardless of their title or position. Create a shared language and knowledge base. Unnecessary hierarchies can stifle flow, so model the change you want to see by being approachable to *all* your employees, no matter where they are on the institutional ladder.

Encourage risk-taking.

Without risk, there's no reward. Create a work culture that encourages risk-taking, so employees feel trusted and empowered to think outside the box and be the best version of themselves. Before you know it, you'll have an office full of superstars working together for the good of the business.

The word "Flow" might be a new concept, but these ideas are time-tested. Buddha achieved ultimate consciousness—and what is that if not flow? Many inventors, including America's greatest inventor, Thomas Edison created breakthrough ideas using these techniques. A McKinsey and Co. study found that top executives are 500% more productive when they're in a flow state. If the "Flow" is this powerful at the top, think about how powerful it can be when multiplied by your entire workforce. If you want to see your business grow, it pays to focus on flow.

Stress and Performance at Work

At first glance, it might seem that flow and stress are polar opposites. You might think that a person under stress would feel so anxious and tight that they could never enter the state of ease and confidence that characterize the flow state. But as the example that opened this chapter showed, stress and flow aren't nearly as far apart as they might at first seem.

In fact, some healthy stress can even help encourage flow. Think of it this way: without a minimum of friction, your car's tires can't propel the vehicle forward. Where there's no friction at all—on a patch of ice, for instance—your car will either find it difficult to start going or will spin out and veer in an unforeseen direction. Just like the friction that makes driving on a highway possible, stress at work makes it possible to get into a state of productive flow.

The word "stress" has a negative connotation. But when you think about it, some stress is unavoidable in most of our daily life. Stress and stress response and are essential elements of work and life. To use the example of driving again, if you don't feel a minimal level of stress when you are behind the wheel, you might get complacent and start driving sloppily. Likewise, in the workplace, without a reasonable level of *healthy* stress, your employees will not feel alert and motivated enough to thrive. Within limits, stress can promote focus. And that focus can sharpen our sensory systems, improve our performance, and help us react to threats engaging our "fight or flight" response, which is key to survival. It must be said here that *too much* stress—in life and in the workplace—can absolutely be a terrible thing. This is important to keep in mind because as the leader of your business, office, or group of employees, you need to create an environment with the right level of stress. Your business cannot be effective if you're so hands-off that your employees don't feel compelled to do their jobs. On the other end of the spectrum, your office cannot thrive if your employees are so stressed out that they're calling out sick every week because they're afraid to come into the office.

So, what is the right level of stress in a workplace? What is the level of stress that will motivate employees without causing them anxiety? To answer this question, let's start by looking at an entirely different area of study: research on marriages. According to relationship researcher John Gottman, the magic ratio of positive to negative interactions is five to one. What does this mean? This means there must be five positive feelings or interactions for every negative feeling or interaction between partners. Stable and happy couples share more positive feelings and actions than negative ones.

If we apply this lesson to the workplace, the bottom line is that you should make sure your employees feel five positive feelings to one negative emotion in the office. For example, if an employee isn't meeting the goals, you set out for them, you can offer gentle criticism, which is likely to be perceived as negative. But to make sure the employee doesn't feel too stressed, make sure that throughout the workweek, you have five positive interactions with the employee—by praising them for a job well done or saying hello and make them feel appreciated.

While Gottman's research provides a valuable template for managing human relationships in your workplace, we can get more specific by looking to research on stress in the workplace. Psychologists Robert M. Yerkes and John Dillingham Dodson studied the relationship between stress and performance in the early twentieth century. They found that *some* stress can actually increase the level of performance. Beyond that optimal level, though, stress becomes counterproductive, and performance falls off.

Stress Performance Curve[3]

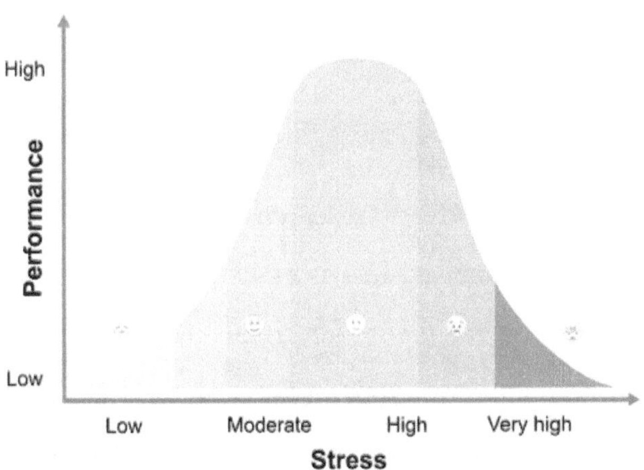

You can promote the optimal stress level in your workplace by implementing the following recommendations from the *Harvard Business Review*:

---

[3] Inspired by Yerkes Dotson Stress Performance Curve

Let your employees feel in control.

Research shows that employees who feel more in control feel less stressed than those who lack control in their workplace. You can help your employees with this by allowing them to have more autonomy at work. If their day-to-day work is mainly self-directed—and directed toward manageable goals—they are likely to feel the right level of "motivating stress."

Help foster authenticity at work.

If workers feel they can't be their "true selves" in the workplace, they will likely handle the responsibility better. You can create an environment that promotes authenticity by asking employees to contribute their ideas and solutions rather than handing them down from above.

Use rituals and rewards.

There's an entire body of research on the power of ritual in enhancing sports performance. Just as a star quarterback has his rituals before a big game, you can create fun rituals in the office: it could be a pizza lunch where you brief your workers on the week's goals or an after-work party to celebrate a job well done. Rituals and rewards can help take the stress off.

Drive and Motivation

As we have seen, one way to create group flow in your office or workspace is to promote high performance through manageable stress. While this is undeniably a key component of flow—and one that every business owner and manager should be aware of—it is also important to understand the underlying motivations of your workforce. There are two types of motivations primarily - extrinsic and intrinsic.

Extrinsic Motivation

Here, we will look at the various drivers of motivation in the workplace, beginning with extrinsic incentives. As we all know, one of the primary motivators of work is compensation: we go to work at least partly because we want to be rewarded monetarily. Compensation also includes less tangible but no less important pieces, for example, benefits like health care and paid time off, as well as the prospect of career growth. All the businesses and organizations in the world want to be profitable and minimize their overheads—this is one common denominator seen in any organizational structure or industry. So, when I bring up compensation, you might be thinking, "I just can't increase my labor cost." But stay with me.

The paradox is that if you genuinely want to reduce your overhead cost, consider paying more than the industry's average wage. This might not make sense at first glance. But paying above the industry average is perhaps the best way for you to secure a motivated and skilled workforce. And a motivated and skilled workforce is a workforce that can flow together—meaning they can help you grow your business.

There is a body of research backing this up. Nobel laureate George Akerlof and Robert Shiller published a book in March 2011 called *Animal Spirits: How Human Psychology Drives the Economy, and Why It Matters for Global Capitalism.* In the book, they describe how fairness in compensation affects both the employer and the employee. The wage that workers deem fair is always above the market-average wage. This is one reason why wages tend to remain sticky even during economic downturns when the unemployment rate goes up. The lesson from this research is clear: your employees will be happier and more motivated—more likely to get into a flow state— if you increase their wages, even slightly. Just by increasing the salary by 10 to 15 percent, you will be surprised how much your organization can save by reducing turnover. As I described in the introduction to this book, the cost of employee separation or employee turnover is at least 20 percent of an employee's annual salary, which reduces your profit significantly. Yet, it is not reflected in most of the financial statements.

There is much to be gained—in terms of employee happiness, reduced turnover, and increased productivity—from increasing wages. It pays to think long-term.

Intrinsic Motivation

Perhaps you work for a business or organization that simply cannot afford to increase labor costs. If that's the case, there is still much you can do to improve your employees' motivation. That's where intrinsic motivation comes into play.

Intrinsic motivation refers to behavior driven by internal rewards—wanting to do a job for its own sake. The focus here is on the sense of accomplishment and pleasure an employee gets from doing the work. How can you increase intrinsic motivation in the workplace? Start by understanding what makes each of your employees' tick. Some employees might have a genuine passion for the industry in which they're working—they might feel internally motivated to advance the cause of your business. Other employees might get fired up about individual tasks—such as writing, delivering an impressive presentation, or working in a small group. The key is to know what motivates everyone in the organization and offer them opportunities to do the work they love.

Another terrific way to motivate your employees is to invite them into the process of collective goal setting. If you get everyone's input on the organization's goals, you'll have their buy-in, and they'll feel compelled to help the organization meet its goals. Similarly, involve employees in day-to-day decision-making to increase the sense of purpose they feel at work.

Next, make sure to provide feedback. Employees who feel that they're doing a good job and recognized for doing good work are likely to feel pleasure at a job well done. Besides the periodic feedback you give yearly or quarterly, you may consider creating an instant peer or cross-business reward program where anyone can give (or nominate) their peer or an individual contributor from a different group a non-contingent award of a small amount. While a manager's feedback is important, your employees also need social feedback, which affects them at an emotional level. Serotonin comes from the recognition of their peers. It creates feelings of power, self-esteem, inner satisfaction, confidence, and a sense of purpose.

Finally, as I mentioned above, increasing employee autonomy is another key driver of intrinsic motivation. Freedom encourages self-confidence and creativity. Daniel Pink, in his bestseller book *Drive*, breaks down these essentials of Autonomy into the 4 T's, as outlined in the chart below. You want to give your employees the freedom to choose what tasks to complete, which team they want to work with, how much time it takes to accomplish the task, and the technique by which they'll get the job done.

The Four Ts of Autonomy [4]

The Four Ts of Autonomy	
Tasks	What tasks to complete.
Team	Which team they want to work with.
Time	When each task needs to be completed.
Techniques	The technique by which they'll get the job done.

It may not always be feasible to give your team autonomy in your business's day-to-day operations and given your industry's competitive pressure. And not every employee will take their autonomy and run with it. In the words of Emma Goldman, "*People*

---

[4] The concept is from the Daniel Pink's famous book - *Drive*

have only as much liberty as they have the intelligence to want and the courage to take." Not all businesses and groups can afford the luxury of giving autonomy to their independent contributors.

But if you think creatively, you might be able to give enough autonomy to your workforce to see remarkable results. Consider creating a program where employees can use 15% to 25% of their time to have some autonomy level, when they can choose the Ts (Task, Team, Time, and Technique)[5] described above. You will be surprised what they come up with.

Some of the best, most world-changing inventions were developed under similar autonomy and creativity-driven structures. Examples abound, from Gmail to Post-It notes, the microwave to Coca-Cola, Dynamite to Matches, Vaseline to tea bags, safety pins to bubble wrap, penicillin to the x-ray machine and implantable pacemakers. No one invented these because someone told them what to do—but try to imagine the world without them.

It's surprising what miracles autonomy can produce. Autonomy can give someone without any particular background or expertise the ability to change the world. In my interview with Naveen Jain, a self-made billionaire, he shared with me that when he started the company Moon Express, he had a fresh perspective. He had no prior experience with space technologies, but he always looked at the details with curiosity. Moon Express was the first company to receive U.S. government approval to send a robotic spacecraft beyond traditional

---

[5] The four Ts of autonomy is described in Daniel Pink's book, *Drive*

Earth orbit and to the Moon. Without autonomy, his dreams never could have become reality.

Passion, Persistence, and Consistency

Motivation, as we have seen, is important for a successful workplace. But motivation alone isn't enough to ensure excellent execution. Passion is important, but it must be paired with persistence and consistency to ensure success.

If you were interviewing someone for a job and say they are "passionate" about doing what your company does, would you hire them without learning their track record and assessing their caliber? Of course not. You would also try to make sure they're persistent and consistent about their work. What you want to look for in employees is, in a word, "grit." Grit is what turns passion into performance. Grit is what makes it possible to work through tough challenges. An "organizational grit" is the glue that holds your workforce together to accomplish greatness despite difficulties. You can develop a spirit of organizational grit by accomplishing challenges as a team. And you can increase determination by instilling these values in your group:

No pain, no gain: your employees—and your business—will not excel unless you work through difficulties.

Embracing challenges: expect that obstacles will come your way, but don't let them stop you.

Discomfort is OK: there's nothing wrong with feeling a reasonable amount of discomfort in the workplace, as long as it spurs you to be your best self.

Turn "can't" into "can": self-limiting beliefs are grit-killers, so encourage a can-do spirit in the face of challenges large and small.

If you fall, get up again: Embody this mindset in your team. Every failure is only temporary, and we can all learn from our past mistakes to become better.

Increasing organizational grit will lead to success and growth. Psychological research tells us that people believe that their most basic abilities can be developed through dedication and hard work. This is the growth mindset. Your employees' intelligence and talent are just the starting point. Fostering a growth mindset creates a love of learning and resilience essential for individual accomplishment and group success. What can we learn from the mindset of high achievers? For that, I turn to poet and TED speaker Richard St. John, who undertook ten years of research and five hundred face-to-face interviews. This research led him to a collection of eight common traits in successful leaders around the world.

Passion: Love what you do.

Work: Really hard.

Focus: On one thing, not everything.

Push: And keep on pushing yourself.

Ideas: Come up with some good ones.

Improve: Keep improving yourself and what you do.

Serve: Serve others something of value.

Persist: Because there is no overnight success.

As a leader in your workplace or organization, you can model these traits and inspire your employees to embrace them. Lift up and celebrate employees who practice grit, and never forget that it takes passion, persistence, and consistent hard work to achieve success.

Why All Your Projects Are Always Late and Over Budget

(And, What to Do About It)

So far, we've seen how important flow is to the workplace, and we've looked at ways that persistence, autonomy, and healthy stress (physiological or mental arousal) can increase group performance. Despite all that, what good is your team's momentum and motivation if you still can't complete a project on time and within the budget? Many factors are unavoidable—it's the way that businesses handle (or do not handle). These practices are some of the main reasons our projects are always late and often go over budget. From my experience as well as the managers and executives I have interviewed from SMBs to Fortune 100 companies and government organizations, here are six ways to help keep your projects on track and within budget:

1. Plan, plan, plan.
2. Remove rose-tinted glasses.
3. Avoid coordination neglect.
4. Resolve strategic dissonance.
5. Reduce information overload.

6. Add contingency cushion.

Plan, plan, plan.

Psychologist and behavior economist Daniel Kahneman writes about the "planning fallacy," which happens when we underestimate the time a project will take, knowing that other projects have taken longer. When laying out a plan—for a quarter, workweek, or workday—start by focusing on "activation energy." If you can motivate your workforce to get ahead before they tackle their work, they'll be able to keep their focus in check and weather any storms— or distractions when the real work happens. Next, guide your employees to first experience the instant gratification that comes from completing smaller, more manageable tasks while they devote more time to longer projects. Finally, to avoid the planning fallacy, you need data. Look back at previous projects and how long it took your employees to complete them to get a realistic idea of how long this next batch of projects will take.

In my interview with a Software Development Manager at Google, Ishwar Joshi revealed interesting approaches Google follows for their product development. Google has a strict project management approach. Comparable projects are taken into consideration employing time and feature-based releases compared using empirical data. Since Ishwar has also worked for other Fortune 100 companies in the past, he said here in Google they don't just "preach" about these project management and planning approaches but they "practice" closely. Unlike many other companies where the project planning and practices are followed top-down, Google's product development team follows these practices bottom-up. Creating this level of planning autonomy and culture can be risky, so they support it with strong collaboration and peer-feedback practices.

I am not advocating one planning approach versus another. Whether top-down, bottom-up, or bi-directional planning is a good fit for your organization? You, as a leader, need to determine the best model that depends on the nature of your business and the resources available.

Remove rose-tinted glasses.

Humans tend to have an "optimism bias," meaning that our brains process positive expectations more readily than negative ones. It's natural for us to do this because it reduces anxiety. On the other hand, too much optimism can give us an unrealistic picture of what is possible in a given time frame. My former colleague used to remind me that the company pays us for our pessimism. Our group was responsible for designing a network in a way to avoid a single point of failure. In this case, as in many other jobs, pessimism can be a virtue—think of jobs in public safety, cybersecurity, and law enforcement, for example. The bottom line is, don't be overly confident when planning.

Avoid coordination neglect.

Coordination neglect refers to a common workplace phenomenon: where people are better at dividing labor than they are at coordinating or integrating their separate pieces of individual work. Researchers Chip Heath and Nancy Staudenmayer have studied this problem and found that the key driver of coordination neglect is poor communication. Fortunately, that's where good leadership comes in. By communicating clearly—across areas of expertise and organizational hierarchies—you can put the workplace puzzle together to ensure the entire business is working to accomplish macro-level tasks on time.

Resolve strategic dissonance.

Strategic dissonance happens when all the stakeholders are misaligned with the priorities of a business or organization. Sometimes factions will emerge, or different segments of your organization will have their own agendas that clash with the organization's overarching goals. Again, this is where skillful communication is invaluable.

In my interview with Mayor Paul Voelker of Richardson, Texas, he pointed out a profound perspective on conflict and consensus while discussing governmental organizations. He said, "When a decision needs to be made, and there is conflict, it helps to get to the bottom of the issues and to understand why people, departments, or organizations are having difficulty agreeing. Constructive conflict allows everyone to understand that there might be underlying issues that they may not even be aware of. But when you pull those issues out, everyone is better able to understand the situation and collectively make wiser decisions. Conflict is important in increasing the level of understanding so you can gain consensus." Mayor Voelker's takeaway has profound implications for your business: embrace constructive conflict. Avoiding it will only make strategic dissonance worse. Bring all stakeholders together, hear them out, and resolve problems before they affect productivity.

Reduce information overload.

When you're trying to make the trains stay on schedule, so to speak, it can be helpful to step back and ask yourself whether you're overloading your employees with unnecessary information. Distraction after all is a killer of productivity. We've all had those days when it's impossible to get into a productive flow because of a million tiny distractions that break your concentration. There are two ways to reduce information overload in workplaces. First, to eliminate unnecessary email communication. Second, think long and hard about whether meetings are necessary. Be mindful that every email, and every meeting, has the potential to derail your group's flow that you've worked so hard to achieve. Another way to eliminate this problem is to let employees' work speak for itself. Employees often feel they have to do two jobs: the work itself *and* justifying or explaining the work they've done. If employees feel they need to spend time justifying their work, that will hold them back from working on the next task.

Add contingency cushions.

You can diligently implement steps one through five, but the unexpected is bound to happen. It's the unknown bumps that can seriously derail your group's momentum. For a project to account for the unexpected, budget for a time cushion, anywhere between 15% and 40% (depending on your industry and nature of work). Unpleasant surprises will happen, but if you've factored that time into your planning, you can cushion the blow.

Measure Optimal Group Performance—Beyond Numbers

In this chapter, I showed why flow is so powerful in the workplace, and we looked at ways to maximize it. We also reviewed ways to harness intrinsic and extrinsic motivation in the workplace. If you've come this far and have implemented my suggestions, congratulations! You are well on your way to a workplace that promotes peak group flow.

Now is the hard part: maintaining these conditions and mitigating any problems that interfere with them. To do this, you have to start by measuring optimal performance or flow. ***If you can measure it, you can manage it*** is an age-old business adage, and it's as true today as it ever was. Venture capitalist James Slavet laid out five new management metrics that can help you maximize workplace flow, and they're worth considering here.

Flow state percentage.

Slavet suggests that 30 to 50 percent of your employees' workdays should be spent in the flow state. That might seem difficult to achieve, but it's possible. To measure your workers' flow state percentage, ask them to track their work over a week and add up the number of hours they're in the flow state. Then divide that number by the hours in their workweek. If they're well under the benchmark, go back to the drawing board and implement more suggestions outlined in this chapter.

Anxiety-boredom continuum.

As we saw earlier, if there's too little stress, your employees will get bored; if there's too much stress, they'll get anxious. Check in with your employees to gauge where they are on the continuum and adjust, as necessary.

Meeting effectiveness score.

Another point we discussed is how meetings can kill concentration and productivity. To measure whether your meetings are necessary, at the end, ask attendees of the meeting to rate the effectiveness on a scale from 1 to 10. If your employees' feedback suggests there's meeting overkill, then consider scaling back.

Compound weekly learning rate.

Employees constantly learning are also continuously challenging themselves and innovating. Even a learning rate of 1% of new material each week can add up. So, ask your team whether they got marginally better or learned something new this week. If they haven't, you might need to give them more challenging work.

Positive feedback ratio.

Earlier, we discussed the importance of giving five times as much positive feedback as a negative one. This is a metric you can measure in your management work. Ensure that for every piece of negative feedback—including criticism, even when warranted—you give five pieces of positive feedback. Happy employees are productive employees.

Think of these five metrics as your flow-management toolkit. With these measurable metrics, you can determine whether you're doing your job to promote individual and group flow in your workplace.

At the heart of workplace, the most important tools available to you for employee engagement is - creating an environment for "Flow" (or momentum) and harnessing the right motivation (intrinsic and extrinsic). Engaged employees are empowered employees, and flow is contagious. Creating a sense of authenticity, offering timely feedback, and removing obstacles to concentration will allow you to create the right motivation for your team. As you create the right conditions for your workforce to flourish in flow and right motivation, you'll see your projects are on track more often, and your organization will become even more innovative and successful.

As Janice Yau famously said, "Teams that flow together grow together."

Chapter 4

Relationship Building and Stakeholder Engagement

"Business is all about relationships, how well you build them determines how well they build your business."

—Brad Sugars

When we look at accounting measures of financial health, we forget to consider some crucial aspects of business performance. Employee and customer retention and stakeholder engagement create value and serve as assets to any organization. Unfortunately, many businesses today neglect these issues to the detriment of their success. All the CEOs and executives I interviewed said that some of the major business problems are customer retention, employee engagement, and relationship building across the board. This chapter will demonstrate how leaders can leverage their emotional intelligence to tap into their most valuable resource—people.

Relationships are essential in your personal life, so why wouldn't they be in your professional life as well? Our relationships with family and friends make us feel safe in our personal lives and help us deal with stress and other difficulties. In business, too, relationships can help ensure the long-term success of your enterprise. At heart, relationships are all about bringing people and resources together to create values. Relationship building in business can help you get new customers, retain customers, reduce customer churn, and manage your reputation.

Sometimes, people confuse relationships with mere compatibility. Compatibility implies that you don't have to work hard once in a relationship because the bond has already been made. This is not how relationships work, as you know from your personal life. **Every relationship demands deliberate efforts and continuous nurturing.** Every relationship is a living organism that requires steady nourishment to thrive. Building, strengthening, and maintaining business relationships involves strategic thinking and planning. This is vital to your business because "your network is your net worth," as the saying goes. The true measure of the success of your business is the strength of your relationships with people in your network.

When we think of starting a business relationship, what comes to mind? In an interview, more than half of 300 senior marketing executives surveyed said event marketing is the discipline that best accelerates and deepens relationships with target audiences. Sometimes though, these events are crowded, making it difficult to forge a meaningful relationship. People exchange cards, put them in their pockets, and move on to the next guest. I want to suggest that forging more meaningful relationships is key to customer acquisition and retention. I lived in Singapore for some time, and I often noticed a gesture that speaks to a deeper form of engagement. For example, I'll use my meeting with Thomas. When I presented Thomas with my business card, he received my card with both hands. At first, I thought this was odd, but the more I thought of it, I realized this showed that

Thomas was being respectful and engaging. Next, he took a good long look at my card and wrote some notes on the back before he put it in his pocket. Noticing the address on my card, he started a conversation about the business complex where I work. I never forgot that encounter because he created a lasting relationship by paying attention and showing interest. This is the power of deliberate but straightforward gestures that can help in relationship building.

Customer Relationship in the Age of Digital Transformation & AI

In my interview with Shep Hyken - a customer service and experience expert, he shared revealing truths in the industry. Hyken is a New York Times and Wall Street Journal bestselling author. These days businesses focus on systemizing the relationship (CRM, IVR, Gadgets, Apps) so often that they forget the primary purpose. I asked him what specifically he'd like to recommend to today's leaders in the digital and AI age. He told me that businesses need to automate the process, no doubt. But anytime in the customer engagement process, when customers need to talk to your staff, they should be able to with no resistance. Your staff may even suggest a digital experience to customers, which is fine, and the clients may not need to talk to the team after doing business for a while, but when they need to connect with a human - it must be easy enough.

He reminded me by quoting notes from his bestselling book "I'll Be Back" - "In the digital age we're in, it's easy to let websites, chatbots, and artificial intelligence take over. Don't become so enamored with the tech that you dehumanize the company. Very few companies have been able to create loyalty with a 100 percent digital platform. (Amazon and Zappos – now owned by Amazon – are two of the few.)." He explained to me you can't automate relationships, but you can automate the process. He shared one crucial point that not many companies consider. When you introduce a new tool or technology internally for customer service, you need to think will make the process easier or harder? If you create friction internally, it will be felt outside by the customer.

He emphasizes building an emotional connection as part of a business's customer experience. To create a rich customer service and experience culture from the top down, leaders must develop values and vision they can share internally and externally (if they choose to). A leader must often communicate and train their workforce for the value and vision. He advocates three steps: define the customer experience vision, communicate often, and train for the vision sustainability across the board in the company. Someone in IT may perceive the vision differently than the people in the warehouse or front-line staff. Even though they may have different responsibilities, they would have the same common language and common goal reflecting the core customer relationship values.

Hyken shared surprising statistics with me from a survey of 1,000 consumers he and his team conducted. I think it's very revealing. You may find it interesting and helpful –

- 79% of Americans trust a brand more if they deliver an excellent customer service experience.

- 87% of Boomers compared to 73% of Gen Z believe it is essential for a company or brand to provide an excellent customer service experience.
- 64% of Millennials compared to 44% of Boomers say great customer service is more important than price.
- 73% of Americans would be willing to go out of their way to go to a company that has better customer service.
- 61% of Americans are willing to go through the trouble of switching brands or companies because of just one very bad customer service experience.
- 52% of Americans will pay more if they know they will receive great customer service.
- 60% of Gen Z compared to 44% of Boomers think companies need to rely on technology to deliver an excellent customer service experience.
- 74% of Americans are likely to recommend a brand or company to friends & family if they provide a convenient customer experience.
- 67% of Americans think ratings and reviews are going to be more important to them in the future.
- 75% of Americans are more likely to be loyal to a company or brand that delivers a personalized customer service experience.

Hyken pointed me to his survey result he has published in one of his articles that shows surprising numbers about customers who will switch because of bad customer service.

Revealing Customer Survey Report

He and his team's survey also revealed one positive result: "Over half will pay more for great customer service." You may consider this a great opportunity and competitive advantage if you are committed to growing your business. He further explained, "More motivation!

Simply put, customer service and a good Customer Experience ("CX") are table stakes. If you don't deliver, you risk losing customers. We asked if the customer would pay more if they knew they would receive great customer service. Fifty-two percent said, "Yes." And 70% would pay more if that service were convenient. That means over half of your customers put service over price, emphasizing that price is less relevant."

Hyken and his team got specific and asked, "For each industry, how much more are you willing to spend for their products or services if you know the company or brand has an excellent customer service experience?" One in four customers is willing to spend up to 10% more in almost every industry if they know a company has excellent customer service.

How Much More is your Customer Willing to Spend

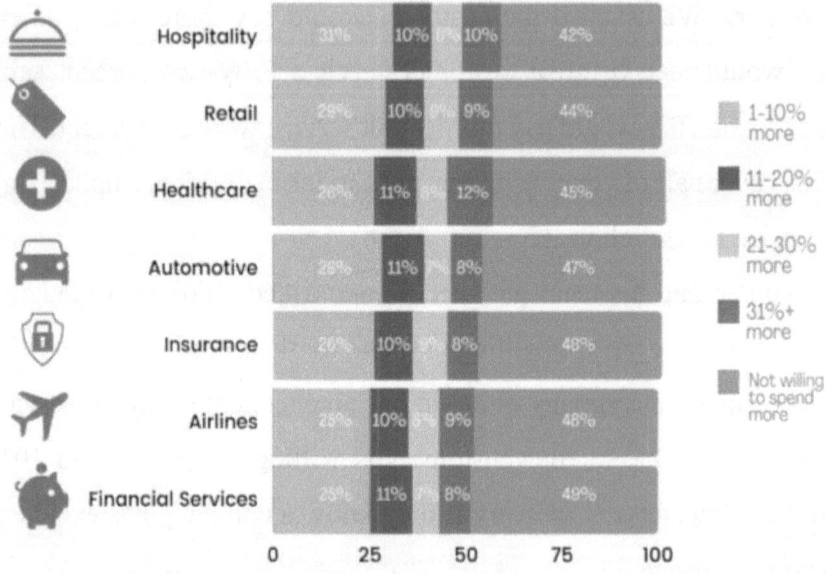

As you have seen from these research and surveys, customer service and relationships can be a major competitive advantage for your business and provide a substantial growth opportunity. You can systemize the relationship in a way, it will be difficult for your competitors to reproduce the same level of customer relationship with the resources you have. I will discuss more in this chapter.

Techniques to Retain Your Customers and Grow Clientele

"Customer Relationship Management" is not just about using software or a tool or a technique—it's less about "management" than it is about the "relationship" part. It's about building rapport and maintaining relationships. Good customer relationship management will include a customer retention strategy to identify ways to entice customers to re-engage through repeat purchases and referrals. Think how many of your prospects or customers go all the way through these phases: Like -> Trust -> Try -> Buy -> Repeat -> Refer.

> **Like**: Do they like your product or service, and do they believe in what you do?
>
> **Trust**: Do they trust your business or brand?
>
> **Try**: Are they willing to try your product or service, even if it's a free trial?
>
> **Buy**: How many of your prospects convert into paying customers?
>
> **Repeat**: How many come back and repurchase?
>
> **Refer**: How many of your customers refer others to your business?

The most effective way to maximize the sustainability of your business is to nurture your relationships with your customers. Successful companies don't just communicate with prospects and customers to promote their products and services. They consistently educate their channel partners, prospects, and customers. Focus on adding value and enhancing your brand and position against your competition. "Communication is the key" is an old cliche, but it's very accurate when it comes to customer service. Here are the seven relationship-building strategies for what to do (and what not to do) that will help you transform your company into a valuable resource for your customers and cement lasting relationships with them.

1. Consider what you communicate.
2. Consider how often you communicate.
3. Encourage two-way communication.
4. Conduct customer interviews.
5. Gather customers' feedback.
6. Assign a relationship manager for your key customers.
7. Offer multiple methods of contact.

Consider what you communicate.

Think about how many marketing and promotional emails you receive in a day. And how many postal mails do you receive? What makes you open an email or letter? Relevance and personalization are the most critical aspects that turn spam into messages that customers open and engage with. If you have 5,000 subscribers, it is useless if they don't open the emails, you send them. Instead, if you have only 250 active subscribers and they all are engaged and interested, your campaign will be more effective. In your communications, try to combine email, direct mail, phone calls, and face-to-face meetings to keep your relationships fresh and strong.

Consider how often you communicate.

How often do you contact customers? Do most of your communications focus on your product or service offers? For best results, it's essential to communicate frequently and vary the types of messages you send. The exact frequency you choose depends on your industry and seasonality, and there is no right answer as long as you don't overdo it. Excessive email frequency is the number one reason people unsubscribe from email communication, followed by the wrong audience, irrelevant content, and lack of personalization.

Encourage two-way communication.

When it comes to customer relations, listening is as essential as getting out your message. Use every tool and opportunity to create interaction, including requests for feedback through your website, surveys (both digitally and using interactive voice response), blogs, and forums. Customers who know they are heard instantly feel a rapport with your company. Working at Microsoft, I realized that collecting customer feedback was essential to every team when developing core features in software development. Everyone in the company was actively engaged in gathering customer responses. You may follow up during the interview to get more information ("Tell me more"). The most important thing to remember is, you're there to listen with an open mind and let the customer do most of the talking. Your customers will appreciate that you have taken the time to engage with them and listen to their feedback.

As a general practice, pause before answering if someone asks you a question, either in interviews or other settings. Even if you know the answer and are eager to chime in quickly, practice waiting a couple of seconds before responding. This has two benefits. It allows you to gather your thoughts and choose the right words. At the same time, customers will appreciate that you listened and took the time to understand their problem before responding.

Gather customers' feedback.

Customer satisfaction research and surveys, both formal and informal, can provide you with an unfiltered look at how customers view all aspects of your relationship. Keep your surveys short and sweet—quick surveys have high response rates, and the feedback is reliable and actionable. "In-app feedback" in a software product or app is one straightforward way to receive feedback on specific aspects of your product or service. These are particularly useful when launching a new product or service or when you suspect that there may be a problem with a specific function of your product. You may also consider including "in-app feedback" points at places where users might struggle the most or where key actions occur.

Assign a relationship manager for your key customers.

Interacting with customer service representatives—whether it's calling your cable company or a moving service—we've all experienced the frustration of being passed along from one representative to another. This requires explaining your problems and issues over and over again to a new person and leads to customer dissatisfaction. If your business has professional services or consultancy elements, consider assigning a relationship manager, at least for your key customers, if you haven't already. It doesn't matter what you call your relationship manager—account manager, service manager, or any other fancy title. You need to assign a relationship manager to build and maintain relationships with your clients. You need to sit down with your relationship manager and set clear goals. Ensure your customer is also aware of the benefits of being a "key customer" and the benefits of having an assigned relationship manager for them. They'll always speak to the same person, and this person will come to build a relationship with them. This may not be feasible to implement for all kinds of business. Still, at least for companies that involve professional services, your customers will appreciate it, and it will pay off.

Below, I present a list of a typical relationship manager's roles and responsibilities. You can use this during the hiring process or for your internal training or team structuring. You don't always have to go outside of your organization to hire someone who can perform these roles, and you may identify someone who can be a true advocate of your customer within your group. The roles and responsibilities of a relationship manager may include:

- They must understand your customer's business as well as your business.

- They know the value proposition to the customer of your products and services.

- They understand your customer's overall strategy to predict when and where your company can add value.

- They should work like a real estate agent; they absorb emotions from both sides and bring the two parties together. They perform technical analysis and convey the customer's unmet and unarticulated needs to the management.

- They should establish priorities and work with its internal (and external) delivery resources to ensure complete customer satisfaction.

- They should have other emotional intelligence skills described in this book, such as - influence competency, tactical empathy, relationship building.

Offer multiple methods of contact:

Customers may appreciate the ability to reach a company through various channels: email, phone, live chat, blog, forum, and snail-mail. However, the companies that benefit most from the multi-channel approach bring together data from all interactions into a single system. That way, a phone representative has a recent and adequate background, and a sales team member preparing for an in-person meeting already knows which questions have been answered via email. For different businesses, some channels might be more effective than others in reaching their customers. For small companies, you will know how your customers like to be communicated with.

If you use **Customer Relationship Management (CRM)** and data-rich analytics, they may reveal which communication channels are most valuable for your problem resolution, retention, sales, or referral management. That analysis can help a business make more data-backed decisions when efficiently allocating customer service resources.

CRM allows you to focus on your, I, and, because of my opinion, tools and integrate them, so they are not in a silo. This leads to a better **Customer Experience (CX).** Don't just collect data in your CRM but put that data to work for you in building relationships with your customers and prospects. Focus your energy on employees willing to listen and adapt to customers, and build a model based on their good practices to inspire others on your team.

Voice of the Customer (VoC) program is another relationship-building tool that has gained momentum as a strategic asset for most customer-centric business minds and forward-thinking CMOs, CEOs, and customer experience leaders. According to 2016 reports by Forrester, the Chief Marketing Officers whose performances rank them in the top quartile report accessing VoC programs more often than their lower-performing peers. This fact alone shows us how powerful VoC can be in forging meaningful customer relationships.

From my experiences—and I am willing to wager that from your experience as well—I have found that most business establishments believe that they are aware of what their customers want. Unfortunately, despite this belief, too many businesses are often only partly correct or entirely off the mark in their judgments of their customers' expectations. By following the steps, I have laid out above, you will be able to correct any mistakes you're making in communicating with your customers. At the end of the day, these tools will enable you to meet the needs of your customers—not just what you believe those needs are. And that is exactly how you can build a meaningful relationship with them.

Employees Engagement Strategies

Relationship building, of course, doesn't stop with your customers. In fact, if you are focused single-mindedly on building bonds with your customers, you can overlook an equally important target: your own employees. Engaging your employees is not simply a matter of making them feel appreciated. The stakes are higher than workplace harmony and a supportive workplace culture. The reason employee engagement is so important is that building relationships with employees translates to a more productive workplace, and a more successful and sustainable business.

The stakes could not be higher. As I have mentioned in the previous chapter, consider this: according to a survey published by Gallup, only 18% of managers in the US had a talent for leadership skills, including the ability to encourage accountability in the workplace, motivate workers, and build relationships with them. I want to repeat that: *only 18% of US managers excel at building relationships with their employees.* Additionally, an alarming 68% of American employees aren't working to their full potential. The result? Gallup estimates this lack of employee engagement costs the US economy about half a trillion dollars in lost productivity every year. To put this number into perspective, this loss each year is more significant than most countries' GDPs. There are 195 countries in the world today, and only the top 25 countries in the world have a GDP higher than this number—half a trillion dollars. The cost of employee separation or employee turnover is at least 20 percent of their annual salary, significantly reducing businesses' profits. Yet this is not reflected in most financial statements. How long someone stays with a company depends on multiple factors, from salary to love of the work to an emotional commitment to the company. But how hard one works is driven more by personal connection, says the author Ray

Lieber of Gotcha Covered HR. As Lieber advises, managers must develop critical skills beyond hiring, placing, and training staff. The emotional connection referred to previously is a pivotal factor in how driven your employees are to work harder and grow with the company.

Let's take a moment to consider why employees might lose motivation. While it might be tempting for business managers to dismiss underperforming employees as lazy, it's essential to understand why employees become unmotivated so you can ensure this doesn't happen to your team. One of the most prevalent sources of employees' lack of motivation is self-doubt, the belief they simply cannot do what their managers ask. They might feel they don't have enough time, don't have adequate training, or don't have the support of their co-workers and managers. When you encounter this, it is often helpful to avoid challenging the employee or taking the "tough love" approach. Instead, help your employee understand that they are supported and that you believe in their ability to execute the work at hand.

Another common motivation problem stems from negative emotions. Employees who feel fearful or anxious are also to feel unmotivated. Helping these employees through their feelings of inadequacy is the key to unlocking their full talents and productive potential. Consider the following interaction between Jerod, an employee managed by Kathy:

Jerod: I'm sorry, but I don't understand how you expect me to get this done.

Kathy: Jerod, can you tell me what you're struggling with?

Jerod: Well, for starters, I've never done this before. I'm kind of surprised that you asked me to do it, given my lack of experience.

Kathy: I chose you for the job because I know you have it in you to step up and deliver.

Jerod: But I'm struggling even to understand how to approach the problem.

Kathy: Jerod, I'm here for you. Believe me, I wouldn't have asked you to do this if I didn't have complete faith you can get it done. I want you to know that I am here for you whenever you have any questions. You're not in this alone.

What Kathy has done is neutralize Jerod's self-doubts. After this interaction, Jerod walks away with renewed confidence in his own abilities. Just as importantly, he knows he's not in this alone. Where he would have previously been unmotivated due to his doubts about his abilities, after talking with Kathy, he feels supported.

It is imperative for managers always to view their employees in the most positive light. Instead of focusing on the negatives, think about how you can help them accentuate their positive attributes. One excellent way to do this is to share your own tips for success. Allow them to learn from you. Listen actively to reach a deeper understanding of their needs and how you can help them achieve their goals.

Another way to build relationships with your employees is to give feedback. Whether it's in an annual performance review or—even better—a weekly meeting, this is one of the most important things you can do to understand your employees. Sometimes you must praise your employee's efforts and celebrate their successes, but it's undeniably true that sometimes you may also have to give some candid feedback so they can improve their performance. It's hard for all of us to feel like we're wrong, and it's even harder for us to hear that from others. Our brains automatically view criticism as a primal threat to our survival. When you give feedback to your employee, use the "sandwich technique." As Mary Kay Ash, founder of Mary Kay Cosmetics, advises, "Sandwich every bit of criticism between two heavy layers of praise." The sandwich technique involves starting a discussion with positive comments, followed by negative criticism before appreciative words are used to close out the conversation. This makes it easier for employees to receive negative feedback. In my experience, this also makes the conversation more pleasant for both sides. It's also helpful to keep your workplace and business conversation fun and easy. "If you laugh together, you can work together," author Robert Orben has written.

Emotionally intelligent leaders are those who excel at engaging their employees. Remember not to blame your employees for being unmotivated. Instead, view underperforming employees as untapped resources. It is your job as the manager to unlock their potential. By building relationships based on mutual understanding, you can help your employees succeed—and help your company in the process.

Stakeholder Engagement

As this book is being written, "stakeholder capitalism" is becoming a hot new topic of discussion in the business world. As opposed to traditional capitalism that involves maximizing shareholder value, stakeholder capitalism is a system in which corporations are oriented to serve the key stakeholders' interests: customers, suppliers, employees, shareholders, and local communities. Under this system, a company aims to create and enhance long-term value in other stakeholder groups.

As a leader, you need to safeguard the interests of customers, co-workers, and stakeholders. It's unavoidable for business growth you need to create customers and grow your clientele. Generating fresh value for customers is the foundation for generating benefits for all stakeholders. You need a task force to support your customers. But in this process, there are many other things you need to take care of, including safety, integrity, legality, sustainability, and inspiring workplaces. Therefore, it's so important to have an expansive idea of who your stakeholders are.

Let's back up for a moment and revisit what exactly we mean when we talk about "stakeholders"? Among all the definitions, I found the Project Management Institute's definition of Stakeholder to be the most descriptive and complete. According to the PMI, the term "project stakeholder" refers to "an individual, group, or organization who may affect, be affected by, or perceive itself to be affected by a decision, activity, or outcome of a project." This definition reveals that stakeholders can emerge from various efforts: projects, programs, consultation, change management, mergers and acquisitions, marketing, or political campaigns, and more. The critical aspect of stakeholder management is understanding the delineation of work and the purpose behind the effort. As stakeholder capitalism has risen in popularity in recent years, one question executives of companies get asked these days is, "How do you balance the needs of stakeholders and shareholders?" In answering this question, it is revealing to look at the case of American Water for an example, and many companies can relate to this. American Water is the largest and most geographically diverse publicly traded water utility company in the United States. In an interview with the VP of Listing & Services, Chris Taylor, American Water CEO Susan Story, reminded, "Water is a health issue, not just a utility service issue. So, the ability to make sure that water is safe, clean, reliable, and affordable is critically important. That's what separates water utility services from other utility services." On the question of how American Water company balances the needs of stakeholders and shareholder, she responded, "I heard a phrase many years ago that said, the generosity of the word **'and'** and the tyranny of the word **'or,'** and I think it has perfect application here." She went on to explain, "To think that you must either choose to focus on shareholders or focus on customers, employees, communities, is ridiculous. Today, free enterprise in our country gets to the point that we are the best system to do all of those. Purpose matters, people matter, and profits matter, and we can bring all of those together to be good for all. We start with our customers, and we start with our communities to provide clean and safe water— which is the most important thing."

Salesforce CEO Marc Benioff once said - "As a capitalist, I believe it's time to say out loud what we all know to be true: Capitalism, as we know it, is dead." Benioff said CEOs must embrace a broader perspective that includes the wellbeing of all "stakeholders." "We valued stakeholders as much as shareholders," he said. The new capitalism is where your employees, partners, and customers are the stakeholders. We might think of this new capitalism as one that values empathy.

These lessons are profound: businesses don't just serve their customers. They serve their stakeholders, and this category is expansive. It includes society as a whole. The same is true in any industry. When you sit on an airplane, you may not realize it takes an aircraft manufacturing company, for example, Boeing, approximately 13,000 suppliers to operate their business, to make a safe flight for everyone. When you're in the air, you, the customer, are one small part of an economic activity that touches so many people.

Now think about any services and products a company provides. Think about who consumes them directly or indirectly. Customers and employees are essential, of course, but if we apply the lessons of stakeholder engagement, you'll begin to think about whether your business can produce the product or service without the supplier's and vendor's commitments. What about the city or town in which your business is located? In the stakeholder framework, it is important to build relationships not just with customers, not just with employees, but with vendors, local citizens, and the community at large, as well.

Recognizing the importance of stakeholder relationships is one thing, but building those relationships is another. So how can you improve your stakeholder relationships? Here are four pieces of advice for you:

1. "Weak Ties" Improve Your Chances of Success.

We might think of the relationships with our customers and employees as "strong ties." Your company works hard to retain employees and keep your customers loyal. But what about other stakeholders, like acquaintances and the community at large? It's helpful to think of these entities as opportunities to forge "weak ties." Weak ties are those relationships outside of your core group of colleagues and employees who can offer innovative, refreshing ideas that your strong ties might not have considered. This might sound like an oxymoron, but it is possible to have *strong* weak ties. Even though the larger community your products and services touch (even if they're not a direct customer), your company does have a significant impact on the world. By being conscious of how your business affects the world at large, you can operate your business in a way that works for the betterment of the community. What's more, by fostering a vast network of weak ties, you can ensure that your ideas never grow stale and that you're not limited by the feedback of like-minded colleagues and employees.

2. Build a Team to Support Your Initiatives.

In the good old days, people were granted authority with their position; there were steeper hierarchies with cut-and-dry organizational schemes. But in the world of flat structures and matrix connections, authority isn't derived from one's title alone. Authority now has to be built or gained, and it is earned through relationship building and stakeholder engagement. It is important that your employees understand that they are not there to serve the company or its customers alone. They are also there to deliver for all stakeholders.

3. Provide Value and Manage Expectations

This advice certainly applies to your customers, but what does this mean when applied to stakeholders at large? Put simply, it means considering stakeholder views at every stage of the product development cycle so everyone from vendors to customers to the community at large knows what product or service you're delivering. Managing stakeholder expectations means there are no surprises at the end of the cycle: stakeholders know what to expect, and their feedback has been incorporated into your business.

Let's consider how stakeholder relationships happen in the real world. I had the opportunity to Interview Vonco Medical CEO Larry DeVitt about relationship building and stakeholder engagement. Vonco Medical provides new and reconditioned physical therapy, athletic training, and medical equipment to rehabs, clinics, and athletic facilities. In my interview, DeVitt shared his leadership journey about restructuring his company by focusing on employee and customer retention and stakeholder engagement. What he shared with me exemplifies how one stakeholder—say, the employee—affects another—the customer. After buying this company a year and a half ago, DeVitt told me he created a customer service atmosphere. What he meant by this was that everyone in his company is a customer relationship manager. The core value of his company is managing and leading by intention. He shares its bottom-line goal with all his employees, who learn about its operations during training. He shares the lessons about stakeholder engagement with his employees to keep them engaged and eager to carry out his stakeholder-centered mission. As DeVitt empowered his employees with knowledge and insight into business operations, these employees, in turn, help the company provide meticulous "white glove service." The employees effectively translate the value proposition to the customer. "Now our clients are getting the value proposition that they are not getting anywhere in the industry," DeVitt explained.

Vanco Medical has a clear strategy for stakeholder engagement. They use a scorecard system to engage their stakeholders. A balanced scorecard is a strategy performance management tool – a semi-standard structured report that executives can use to track the execution of activities by their internal and external stakeholders and monitor the consequences arising.

While I am not suggesting you follow one particular leadership strategy, I believe that you should have a strategy that engages each employee, not just the executives and managers. What good are the executives and middle managers if their direct reports are not engaged and don't deliver? And, what good is engaging employees if they don't engage other stakeholders—from the customer to the vendor? All stakeholders are interwoven. When we build a relationship, that trickles down and affects our relationships with others.

Common Traps in Relationship Building

Let's face it, we all occasionally come up short when it comes to building relationships with our stakeholders. That's okay—the important thing is to acknowledge our shortcomings so we can improve on them. The goal is not perfection, but instead, we should aim for constant improvement. That said, here are three common traps in relationship building. Knowing these pitfalls will make you better equipped to handle whatever comes your way as you forge deep, lasting bonds with your stakeholders.

Trap 1) Imbalance relationship priorities.

Many business owners don't value their customers as much as they should. And those who appreciate their customers often forget that employees, business associates, and suppliers are equally important. As I described in this chapter, stakeholders are as important as customers to their businesses. Treat your customers like royals and let them know you value and appreciate them. The same is true with anyone else who contributes directly or indirectly to your business. You should achieve a balanced outlook when focusing on the stakeholders in your orbit.

Trap 2) Creating vs. Capturing Values.

Another common trap that gets in the way of relationship-building is being good at capturing value but not creating it or vice-versa. If you're dealing with a stakeholder and thinking, "Let me see how much value I can extract from you," this is generally not going to be a very productive approach. We might think of this mindset as one of capturing value. This is not a great start to a relationship, and it is not the basis for a sustained relationship. Consider the alternative, in which you think, "Let's figure out what you care about and what I care about, where those things overlap and where we can cooperate so that we can help each other." It is necessary to do this with a full awareness you and the stakeholder may occasionally be in tension due to competing needs for the same resources. In reality, we can't have everything. But lets at least maximize what's possible for us to have together.

The reverse problem is being good at creating value but not at appropriately capturing it when required. Some of us are wonderful at catalyzing things, coming up with creative innovative ideas, helping others accomplish their goals. But we might not seize the initiative, and we end up **not** getting credit for a positive outcome. It's not a bad thing to capture value when necessary. Capturing doesn't mean becoming an opportunist. The important thing to remember is that equilibrium is essential. Strive to balance value creation and value capture.

Trap 3) Delay in forming strategic alliances.

This trap results from failing to focus on relationships ahead of time. I like to joke you don't want to be meeting your neighbors for the first time in the middle of the night while your house is burning. It's difficult to do everything at once: when your house is on fire, focus on putting it out! Don't focus on chatting with the neighbors. I often see leaders who tend to focus upwards and downwards at the same time. They focus on building relationships with their bosses and with their direct reports, but they fail to consider laterally. As a result, they delay forming some of those critical relationships with their peers and allies. Later, when they need help, then they will ask their peers for support. "Ah, so now you need me?" —that person might think. The lesson here is that your coworkers—those at the same level in the organizational hierarchy—are stakeholders as well.

The CEO Disease

An alarming number of C-level executives suffer from "CEO Disease." The good news is it's not an actual disease. If you haven't heard this before, "CEO disease" is the information vacuum around a leader created when people withhold important (and usually unpleasant) information. It's a phenomenon that many leaders (not just CEOs) remain isolated from undesirable pieces of information or honest feedback. The larger an organization gets, the less likely it is that unwelcome news will travel smoothly up the chain. If you are a leader in this information age, you are as good as the information you have. The information gap can cause a lack of trust within your organization, external stakeholders, and customers.

First, you have to understand why your employees or stakeholders are filtering such information. They may not be telling you the whole truth for many reasons. They fear being the bearer of bad news. Or they feel it's above their "pay grade" to comment on such topics. Although this "disease" is not real, it poses real business problems— such as employee disengagement, mediocre decision-making due to inadequate input, and dissatisfied customers.

Once you are aware of this information vacuum, the fixes are easy. Create a safe environment and "open door policy" to encourage openness and communication flow up the chain. Ask for feedback and input— you can ask in your team meeting or one-on-one meetings. You will be surprised at what you discover sometimes. If you manage a large organization, you may consider or may already have a "360-degree feedback" policy. A 360 review or feedback tool solicits feedback about an employee from all directions: their managers, coworkers, and direct reports.

Relationships are key in the business world. The difference between a successful business and one that fails often comes down to leaders who build lasting relationships with customers, employees, and the broader universe of stakeholders, from vendors and suppliers to the local community. Emotional intelligence is necessary to build relationships with all stakeholders. By nurturing your relationships with others, you can inspire unmotivated employees, create a loyal customer base, and positively impact the community at large. By communicating effectively, listening with empathy, and avoiding the common traps that prevent relationships from budding, you can put yourself—and your business—in an excellent position to build lasting relationships with everyone you encounter. The key is to build relationships and enjoy your journey along the way.

Chapter 5

Emotional Intelligence in Strategic Sales

"As the Internet has sped up the consumer experience, customer expectations are higher."

—Greg Gianforte

Almost all the CEOs I interviewed, from both large and small companies, stated funnel building, business development, and customer retention are their major challenges for the business, whether or not they are "sales-driven CEOs" or not. To thrive as a business today, you need sales, and to make sales, you need to build the right sales culture. Before we dive into the how-to of building a sales culture, it is worth surveying today's sales landscape. The picture, as we know, is sobering. The Internet, e-commerce, and Artificial Intelligence have already taken over 60% of all sales jobs, just as these trends have affected almost every other job in today's economy.

We know that e-commerce is replacing sales jobs in business-to-customer (B2C) and business-to-business (B2B) sales, particularly in the manufacturing and distribution spaces. Product research and comparison shopping are already done effectively online. Meanwhile, the order process is increasing, if not yet completely, automated by various order management system software platforms. Once the order is taken, automation and system integration can even push the orders to the manufacturing company's order system via Application Program Interfaces (APIs). Not all retailers and manufacturers have fully embraced these technologies yet, but they all will at some point in the near future.

Given these seismic shifts, many business owners and leaders wonder, "How can the more traditional B2B manufacturers and their sales organizations embrace e-commerce and still have a place for traditional sales jobs?" Before you hit the "panic" button, rest assured that these traditional B2B companies will have sales jobs in the future, but they won't be the sales jobs of the past. Whatever business you're in, you will have to adapt to these changes to stay competitive.

The sales force of the future will need to be more "consultative" than the traditional sales team. To make a dynamic, consultative sales team, business leaders must provide salespeople with better education and training opportunities, so they understand the big picture of the market and the nature of your company's competition. Transforming your team from making sales to becoming thought leaders will give your business an edge and ultimately add value for your customers. In this chapter, we'll explore how you can make this happen. While the theories described here can be applied to any sales—traditional, transactional, or strategic, the techniques I explore apply most closely to strategic sales. We will turn to the important question of what strategic sales are.

When you hear "sales," what do you think of? Many of us might think of a salesperson selling a product—a car, computer hardware, or a manufacturing component—to a business or customer. When we think of this salesperson, we probably think of their goal as selling the maximum product to the most customers. This is the sales model we might label "transactional." Such selling focuses on one-time sales, with the ultimate goal of pushing the most product. Retail outlets such as hardware stores and e-commerce companies such as Wayfair are paragons of transactional sales. Automotive dealers and real estate agents too have the same goal, even if the product they're selling is different. When a transactional sale is done, so is the relationship between the customer and the business. The hardware store sells a lawnmower, Wayfair sells a rug, a car dealership sells a Ford, and the realtor sells a four-bedroom home to a family. After that, the deal is done, and the seller and customer go their separate ways.

Strategic sales, also known as complex or enterprise sales, differs from transactional sales. Where transactional sales involve discrete, often one-time purchases, strategic sales involve the entire sales cycle—from requests for proposals to research to bids. There are multiple stakeholders, longer sales cycles, and—crucially— a high degree of risk that the purchaser is taking on when choosing which supplier or company to reward with a contract ultimately. Given these high stakes, this sales process requires the seller to gain the prospective customer's trust.

When it comes to employees, strategic sales require the creation of thought leaders for your business, competitive compensation plans for your team, a workplace characterized by motivation and incentives, and technology investments. Big-picture considerations include a right-sized sales force that is challenged but not overworked. The sales force size affects customers, salespeople, and the overall sales organization, besides the overall profitability of your enterprise. Likewise, sales territories and coverage must be in balance to avoid spending too much money and time on low-potential customers while spending too little on high-potential customers. Because of imbalanced sales territories, sales organizations can leave millions of dollars in lost productivity unrealized.

This table below distinguishes the main differences between transactional sales and strategic sales, and it applies broadly to almost any business.

Transactional vs Strategic Sales

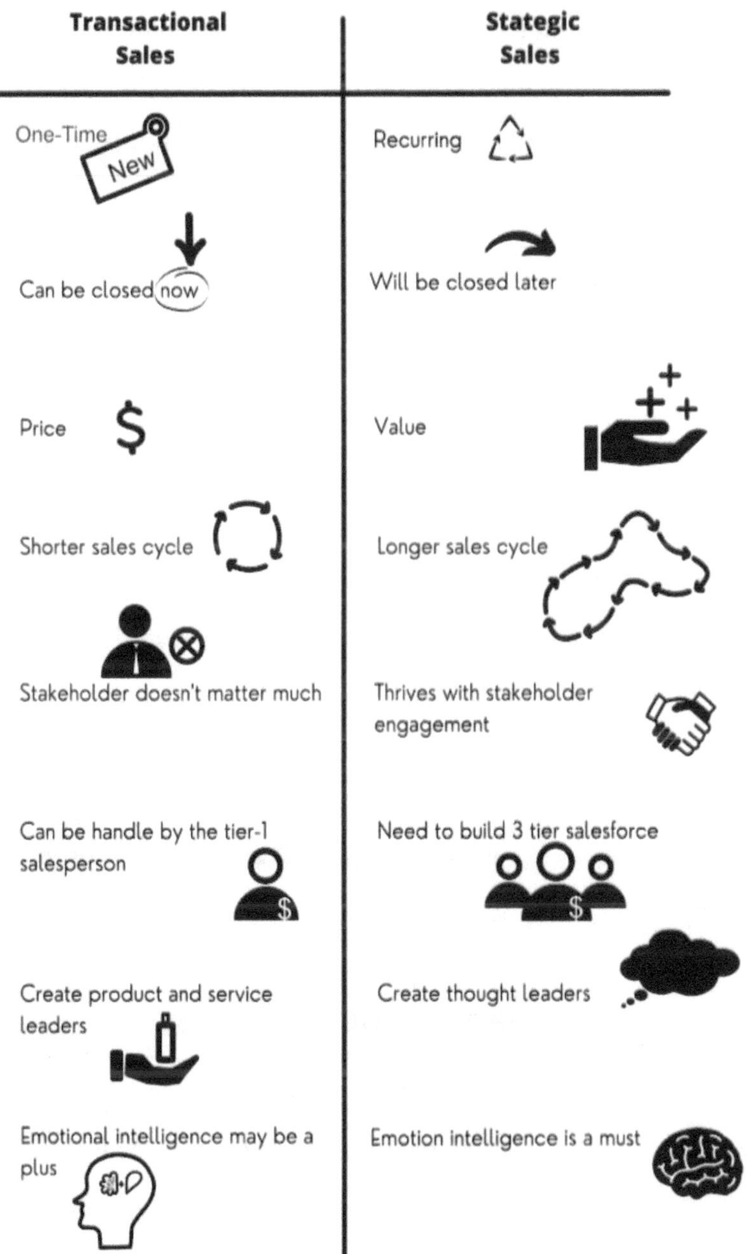

As you can see, strategic sale is a longer-term process than transactional sales. In strategic sales, your customer isn't a passive object you're selling to—they're an active stakeholder in an ongoing process. In fact, which is the key difference between the types of sales: transactional sales have a discrete outcome (to sell a product), while strategic sales are a process (to build a recurring customer base).

Of course, every business leader would prefer a recurring customer base, but how is this done? The key, it turns out, is cultivating a sales force of thought leaders with high emotional intelligence.

In today's business world, the employee's job function in a professional services role is almost always cross-functional. Emotional intelligence empowers employees to imagine new ways to solve existing problems and create tools to make your business better, faster, and smarter. Rather than focusing only on orders or closing, the emotionally intelligent salesperson persuades, convinces, and—above all—influences the customer base to help your business grow. You can think of this as "non-sales selling," and it is all about directly or indirectly influencing people.

The New ABCs of Selling

The 1992 film *Glengarry Glen Ross* gives a classic peek into the sales process as it was conducted back in the day. Alec Baldwin plays Blake, a successful sales manager who visits the struggling real estate agents Mitch and Murray. He is there to reveal the truth about selling. In a flourish, Blake says, "You can't play in a man's game. You can't close them. Then go home and tell your wife your troubles because only one thing counts in this life: get them to sign on the line which is dotted." Blake flips over a blackboard dramatically, which has letters on it: "ABC." Blake goes on to explain, "A: Always. B: Be. C: Closing. Always Be Closing. Always be closing!" Although this was fiction and anecdotal evidence in the literature, such was the sales mindset back then.

The times have changed—both in terms of management techniques and in the reality of sales. In this digital age, information is ubiquitous, as Daniel Pink describes in his book *To Sell is Human*. Pink proposes a redefinition of the law of sales by introducing the new ABC's:

A — Attunement

B — Buoyancy

C — Clarity

Attunement, Pink explains, is "the capacity to take another's perspective, to understand their interests, and to see the world from their point of view." *Buoyancy* is "the capacity to stay afloat in what one salesman calls an 'ocean of rejection.'" *Clarity* is "the capacity to make sense of murky situations, to curate information rather than merely access it, and to move from solving existing problems to finding hidden ones." Pink stresses these three qualities are now essential in your personal life and your business career. Whether you're trying to convince your daughter to do her homework or you're trying to move a prospect to buy a computer system, the new ABCs offer the tools to change mindsets.

This is important to our discussion because, as you can see, two-thirds of the sales process requires sound emotional intelligence. Likewise, for any knowledge-based workers, such as company management, government officers, accountants, lawyers, engineers, architects, doctors, scientists, academics, or any other white-collar workers whose line of work requires them to "think for a living" — emotional intelligence plays a vital role in cross-functional collaboration.

Building an Emotionally Intelligent Sales Culture

The challenge for CEOs is creating a sales force composed of emotionally intelligent people. Emotional intelligence in strategic sales starts with transparency. This might sound obvious, but it is worth considering because transparency is the key to unlocking the potential of any sales situation. When a salesperson is transparent, they have the right to demand transparency. A transparent salesperson should ask customers relevant questions about their interests, budgets, buying processes, procurement timelines, and involved stakeholders. When I am a buyer, and a salesperson brings transparency to the table, they immediately earn my trust, and they have credibility right off the bat.

As I explained in the previous chapter about "Influencing Mindset," **if you make a statement, they listen to them "passively," but if you ask them questions, it will compel them to think more "actively."** Thoughts follow actions. Think about what you're selling and why the client wants to buy it. Then reverse engineer your questions. Maybe your client could save time and money by using a solution you can provide; you can explore what it would mean to your client to save time and money. Every question should elicit an answer that will help you match your solution to their problem areas, pain points, or challenges. Think of it as a human conversation. If you wanted a friend to go on a vacation with you, what questions would you ask them to convince?

Consider these examples when you or your team is trying to qualify a prospect -

"What problem are you trying to solve?"

"What have you tried in the past?"

"Is doing nothing an option?"

"How important is this for your business?"

"Why are you solving this problem now?"

"What is relevant for your business operations today and next year?"

"Why weren't you happy with your last vendor?"

"What other solutions are you evaluating?"

"What are your top priorities in a solution?"

"How quickly are you hoping to see results?"

"What can prevent us from working together?"

"On the scale of 1 to 5, what is the number that shows your willingness to work with our company?" (When they choose a number—say 3 or 4—I would ask, "Why didn't you choose a lower number?" Their answer will promote your company in their words. When they praise your company in their words, their mind listens, and finally, it influences their mindset.)

Let the clients do most of the talking. As they say in sales—the more you talk, the less you sell. Even if your prospect doesn't answer all of your questions, they still provide valuable information when they pause or decline to answer a question.

Strategic sales extend far beyond transparency, though. More science than art, strategic sales entail the vast array of what we might call "mind-games," including how you respond to emails and bids, how you handle objections, and how you move the prospect down into the funnel of the sales cycle. All the salesperson's knowledge about the product, industry, and trends does no good if their brain can't access it quickly when they need it.

Business leaders must train their sales team to quickly handle the objections of prospective customers when pitching your product or services. The thought, "Why didn't I say that to the customer?" — should never enter the salesperson's mind. They should have reacted at the moment to head off any objections or concerns the client raised. The psychological and biological aspects of emotional intelligence discussed in the previous chapter—from nonverbal cues like facial expressions and body language to verbal cues like expressions of empathy and interest in client's needs—are important to consider when we talk about emotional intelligence in strategic sales.

In a sales situation, the mind reacts to a difficult buyer or a sales objection with the same intensity as if our very survival was being threatened. As I'll discuss in the forthcoming chapter *Leading with Mind, Body & Soul*, this is where amygdala takes over our emotions. A small, almond-shaped structure above the eyes, the amygdala is the oldest part of the brain and screens all stimuli coming into the nervous system. This processing happens without logical thought or reasoning. When the "old brain" senses danger, it produces a fight-or-flight response in a person. This part of the brain was more useful some 100,000 years ago, when our ancestors' life expectancy was only about 25 years, and they were constantly hiding from or fighting predators in animals and other tribes. But even today, the human brain cannot help but screen information through the amygdala, which means the fight-or-flight response is at work in the minds of clients when confronted by your sales force.

An emotionally intelligent sales team is invaluable in communicating to customers that they're not dealing with a threat but with a genuine person. Many untrained salespeople unknowingly send prospects into fight-or-flight mode because of their outdated selling techniques. Salespeople who lack emotional intelligence sound defensive and follow up with uptight meetings, get into "chase mode," and ultimately lose clients to competitors.

Another holdover from the old way of selling happens when salespeople ask leading questions they were taught in tactical sales. **Questions like, "So, you want us to demonstrate how our product or services can save you thousands of dollars?"— triggers the amygdala.** The old brain hears the close coming, causing them to throw their defenses up, and the prospect goes into fight-or-flight mode. Prospect responses vary from objections (fight) to "I'll think it over" (flight).

So, what is the best way to handle this? You can train your sales force to use empathy strategically to defuse sales objections before your prospects even bring them up. We'll explore this further in the next chapter, *Empathy—Competitive Advantage in Business*. Here, I'll simply note that when people feel heard, they respond differently. So, one general rule is to ask plenty of relevant questions to understand better what concerns them and how you can meet their needs.

How to Use Emotional Intelligence for Strategic Sales

Let's turn to more specific examples of how you can apply emotional intelligence to strategic sales situations. While each of these examples may not apply to your specific line of business, I hope that they provide an overall picture of how to foster emotional intelligence in your sales force regardless of the nature of your organization.

Recognize emotional triggers.

If you don't understand what might trigger a negative response from a client or prospective customer, you're bound to be surprised when they walk away. By being aware of hot-button emotional triggers, you can ensure that you won't send the wrong message—and the wrong response—from your customers. Ensure your body language, verbal communication, and selling techniques don't send the client into "distrust" mode. If you're open with them, chances are they'll be open with you. In other words, trust people to gain their trust.

The salesperson too must draw on information gleaned from emotional intelligence to make a complex sale. Your goal should be to bridge the gap between emotion and logic to be successful in strategic sales. The magic happens when you pair emotional insights with logical insights. For example, you might have done all the research in the world into your prospective customer's profile. Still, this **logical thinking won't necessarily translate into a sale unless you also draw on what you can know only through emotional intelligence**. Knowing how your prospective customer interacts with people and being aware of their triggers is necessary for creating a meaningful connection.

Delay the gratification of a quick sale.

In strategic sales, delaying the gratification of the immediate sale opens a door to the long-term gratification of customer relationships that can pay off over time. Think about making a sale that will impact your company not just today but next quarter and beyond. Many vendors don't even pursue bigger, strategic deals because it's easier to sell to customer counterparts who are at the same organizational level. Some salespeople simply would prefer to avoid talking to C-level executives and others involved in strategic decision-making, either due to intimidation or not wanting to do the legwork of selling strategically. But this is something you can avoid with your sales force by encouraging long-term thinking.

It's OK if you don't have all the answers.

A big stumbling block with many salespeople feels like they've failed if they don't know the answer to a challenging question a customer pose. Everyone is human and being direct about what you don't know is another way to build trust. Don't worry if you don't answer immediately but be prepared to look into it and get them the response they need. Even if you don't know how to respond at the moment, be confident. If your salespeople don't sound confident about what they are saying, why will the customer believe what they are pitching?

Manage expectations.

There's no surer way to upset your client than by being vague about the nature of what you're delivering or the timeline you'll need—or, even worse, not delivering on what you have promised. **If you want to trigger a positive emotional response in your customer, one of the best ways to do this is to set clear expectations and deliver on them.** During pre-sales set clear expectations of what *you* need from the customer to give them what *they* need. You might need to know, for example, what time constraints they are working under to give them excellent service. Being direct and clear from the start is the only way you can ensure that you're able to deliver what they expect from you.

Although, our focus here is "strategic sales," let's consider this example since regardless of the nature of your business, you can quickly relate this situation with your sales process. Suppose someone is purchasing a home and they have hired a real estate agent to help them in this process. The real estate agent needs to set reasonable expectations for the homebuyer not to walk away dissatisfied. If the buyer expects to walk into the first house, they see and fall in love with it. They will probably end up disappointed. That's why the real estate agent must communicate what the buyer should expect—for example, a three-week process in which they'll visit five homes per week. Similarly, the real estate agent needs to be clear about what they expect from the client. To do their job and meet the buyer's needs, they need the buyer, be honest about what types of houses they do or do not like, what neighborhoods they will and won't consider, and what price point they won't exceed. If the buyer doesn't want to commit to spending this much time house-hunting or isn't open and honest with the buyer, then the relationship shouldn't go any further. And that's OK! Often, not making a sale is an acceptable outcome if the alternative is likely to be a relationship that doesn't satisfy the buyer's or the seller's needs.

Use tactical empathy in strategic sales.[6]

We have all had to deal with customers who are aggressive and demanding. We can't control the customer's initial response, let alone their attitude, but we can control how we respond to their energy. Empathetic salesperson put themselves in the customer's shoes. They think about the pressure their clients are under and the pressure points they can help ease. Often, the elephant in the room is the dynamics in

---

[6] Chris Voss, a former FBI hostage negotiator and co-author of the bestseller Never Split the Difference, coined the term "tactical empathy" to describe the process of trying to understand your opponent on an emotional level to get a handle on challenging situations.

their organization. By asking questions, listening carefully, and, above all, caring, you can use empathy to strengthen the customer relationship.

Be patient.

As your strategic sales plan bears fruit and your business grows, you will have the "good problem" of onboarding new salespeople. During this process, be patient with new sales members and take time to show them the ropes. After all, they may be following the "old rules" of sales, and it will take some getting used to the strategic sales goals you have set for the team. Remind your sales managers of the need to be patient as the new salespeople learn about your products, services, and the nuances of your company and the industry.

Be aware of your customers' biases.

All of us—salespeople and customers alike—have biases. No customer is a blank slate and excelling at strategic sales requires your sales force to be attuned to the biases of your prospective customers. How the customer feels during the sales pitch is more important, I would argue, than the quality of the pitch. The customer might have biases against a particular type of sales technique. Maybe they don't like strong pitches that put them on the spot. Perhaps they just don't like a specific kind of salesperson. Whether the bias is based on gender ("I prefer working with women") or something less definite ("I don't like pushy people"), your sales team needs to use emotional intelligence to gauge the customer's biases and set them at ease.

These biases come from past experiences. **Perhaps the customer**

had an unpleasant experience with a salesperson in your line of work, and now they tend to think of all sellers of a particular product or service as untrustworthy. Perhaps they worked with a competitor and now view your line of business with suspicion. In these cases, your sales team needs to be aware of these negative biases and work to build trust and set your product apart from the competition.

Don't sweat rejections.

In sales, rejection happens. It's nothing personal and getting rejected is no reason to react emotionally. While this might sound easier said than done—no one likes getting rejected, least of all salespeople—there is a lot of sales managers can do to take the sting off rejections.

In strategic sales, take off the pressure of new members of your sales team by letting them know they don't have to sell anything in their first few interactions. During this time, you can help them set realistic expectations about the rejection they're bound to face. Teach them about your industry's and your company's rejection-to-sales ratio and ask them to anticipate that. Estimating how many rejections your sales rep can expect can help immunize them to rejection. And when rejected, which will inevitably happen, level with them by telling them a story about a rejection you've faced. This will help them handle the rejection with emotional maturity.

Selling to the Old Brain

Part of using emotional intelligence in strategic sales involves recognizing what kind of "brain mindset" you're selling to. This might sound strange, so allow me to explain. The human brain has evolved over millions of years, and much of our neurological processing includes the regulation of "old" needs that suited our species in its earliest days. Our old brains are responsible for drives that ensure survival — from avoiding threats to seeking relationships, from increasing status to seeking rewards like food and sex, this old brain is still alive and well in the here and now.

The "new" brain, which developed later in human evolution, is responsible for our ability to use higher reasoning and deduction to help process stimuli and solve complex problems. Underneath this higher brain functioning, though, the old brain is always at work. It is always assessing threats and seeking rewards, as it has throughout all human development.

Often when discussing sales, we think about persuasion and reasoning. We're trying to explain why our product is superior or how we can help them solve a difficult business problem. This is an appeal to our customers' new brains. This is all well and good, of course. When selling, we have to appeal to our customers' higher cognitive functions. After all, it often is quite helpful to draw distinctions between what your business offers that your competitor does not. However, I want to argue that strategic sales involve more than just appealing to customers' new brains. In a complex sale, you have to consider the old-brain motives when your sales team is talking with prospective clients.

When we appeal to the old brain in strategic sales, we seek to build meaningful human connections with our customers. We set them at ease, allow them to trust us and open, and we show our authentic selves. Asking leading questions and "going in for the kill" with a quick sale triggers the old-brain emotion, leading to feelings of unease, mistrust, and ultimately a desire to flee from the situation. That's why it's so important in complex sales to tell customers exactly where you're coming from and what you want, without using trickery, flattery, or subterfuge, all of which will signal to their old brains that you're a threat.

Another way to defuse a negative response from the old brain is to simply be honest. **You can gain the trust of prospective customers by trying to solve a problem *along with them* rather than *for them*.** By that, I mean that not every sales conversation needs to end in a sale. If you think long-term, you can gain customers' trust not just today but for the long haul. Maybe what they need today is *not* to buy your product or service. Perhaps they already have the tools and resources to solve their problem and they don't have any unmet needs right now. If that's the case, build rapport and they will come back to you when they need your help.

People Don't Buy Products and Services—They Buy Feelings and Emotions

Drawing a distinction between new-brain selling and old-brain selling reveals a key insight: your customers are not buying your products and services; they are buying feelings and emotions. You might have heard often: **"people buy on emotion for logical reasons." At first glance, this sounds paradoxical, but it captures how our customers' old brains and new brains interact when we're selling to them**. Our customers make purchasing decisions primarily based on emotions (old brain), and after they have made that emotional decision, they justify their buying decisions with logic (new brain).

If you think about it, this is probably true with your own personal purchasing decisions. Consider the car or house you own. Now ask yourself why you bought that car or that house. Deep down, you probably identify with some aspect of the brand of the car you buy, and emotions associated with that house you bought—and you want to signal that affinity with other people who see you driving or living in that house.

This applies to all of us. We buy specific makes and models of cars because of the way they make us feel. Electric cars have boomed in popularity as this book is being written. Why? A large part of the reason I would argue that is because electric vehicles signal purchasers that they're environmentally friendly, hip, modern, and socially conscious. And when we drive these cars, we in turn signal these traits to others. Examples are endless. Consider the house you live in. Why did you choose to buy *this* house and not a different one? Perhaps you want to be associated with the high status or coolness of a particular urban neighborhood. Or maybe you want to raise your children in an idyllic suburban ranch house. Perhaps you and your partner always wanted to buy a 1920s bungalow in a tight-knit neighborhood. Whatever the specific desire, you're buying more than just the house — you're purchasing the emotions associated with a particular lifestyle, a unique dream of the future.

Underlying the positive feelings we associate with the cars, homes, and literally, everything else we buy is also the need for security. As humans, we all want to feel safe and secure. It's no secret that sales involve relieving customers of their insecurities. The products and services we offer meet the needs and extinguish the anxieties of our customers. **Without the feeling of insecurity, most products and services would not even exist.**

This helps explain why insurance is such a gigantic industry in the US and worldwide. In the US alone, net insurance premiums totaled $1.32 trillion in 2019. People don't buy insurance, they buy certainty. The same is true of virtually any other product or service your business offers: your customers are buying assurance, peace of mind, and security.

Emotional Selling

Research by the Nielsen Company shows that roughly 90% of purchasing decisions are made subconsciously. Think about that for a moment. This means that nearly all of your customers are buying what you're selling based on old brain thinking.

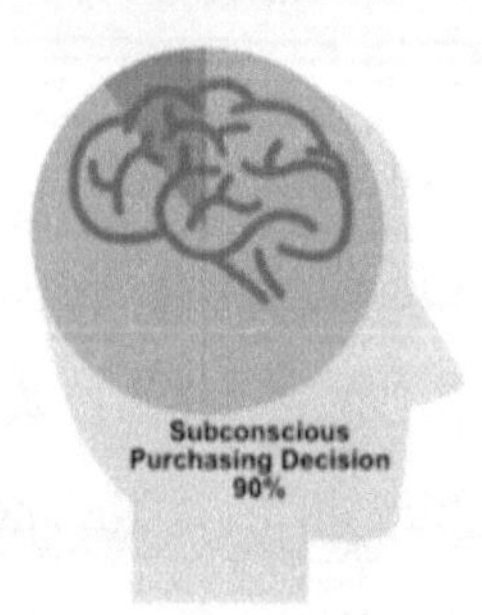

Understanding this—and genuinely embracing it in your company's strategic sales—will open the door to increased revenue and long-lasting customer bonds. **Your customers will respond positively if you harness the power of emotional intelligence to help them perceive the emotional value of what you sell.**

Structuring your Sales Force

When structuring your sales force, along with the subject matter, you need to gauge and emotional intelligence of everyone on your team. A team member with relatively little emotional intelligence will not be the best fit for a position that requires building trust. Likewise, the talents of a salesperson with high emotional intelligence will be squandered if they're serving in a merely transactional role.

Consider a typical three-tiered sales force structure:

Tier 1: Sales Executive

Tier 2: Problem Solver

Tier 3: Trusted Advisor

In tier 1, salespeople are conducting primarily transactional or one-time sales deals. This work usually involves cold-calling prospective clients. Tier 2 involves more hands-on, tailored work for helping customers solve a specific problem. This requires a deep understanding of the client's problems and the ability to offer custom solutions. Tier 3, meanwhile, is responsible for fostering an even greater emotional connection with the client; they have to understand the customer's budget and seasonality.

Emotional intelligence is required for each tier. But it is important to note that the higher the tier, the more emotional intelligence is needed to excel in the role. In tier 3, for instance, the salesperson should create such a deep emotional connection with the customer they don't even view them *as a customer*. They see them as a partner, and the customer in turn, views the salesperson with the same trust. The tier-3 salesperson won't hesitate to walk away without a sale— and that's OK. If your company isn't the best fit to solve their problems, the tier-3 salesperson will recommend solutions that don't involve your company. **Even if the customer doesn't go with your company, your tier-3 salespeople have nevertheless "won" because they have forged a lasting bond.** The prospective customer might recommend your company to other clients, and they might even choose you to address a different problem in the future.

If you want a sales force designed for 100% complex and strategic sales, you need all three tiers. Your responsibility involves identifying those salespeople with the highest emotional intelligence and placing them in tiers 2 and 3 so they can excel at what they do best.

Create *more* Thought Leaders

To increase your business's sales, CEOs need to do more than simply identify talent. They have to *create* more tier-3 salespeople from within the ranks of their staff. By developing tier-3 salespeople, I mean developing thought leaders in your field: people whom prospective customers will look to not just when they want to buy your products and services but when they want information and guidance beyond what your business can offer with a sale.

Developing thought leaders start by creating a culture that promotes strategic sales rather than transactional sales. It involves fostering traits like attunement, buoyancy, and clarity in your sales force. And above all, it consists of fostering a sales culture that sells to the old brain and values emotional intelligence over the old way of doing sales.

The Most Underutilized of all Sales Tools

I invite you to put into practice the ideas and techniques I have discussed in this chapter. But I want to leave you with a final piece of advice. Although important to understand concepts like emotional intelligence and the new ABCs of selling, it is different from practicing these concepts in the real world. And practice is what is required to promote a strategic sales culture based on emotional intelligence. Practice is the most underutilized of all sales tools. Without practicing the tools of emotional intelligence, your sales team will never master them. As I explained in the previous chapter, practice is the key to building neural pathways, and these new neural pathways will make strategic sales second nature for your team. It's just like exercise: you don't get fit by reading about calisthenics, and you don't train for a marathon by reading a guidebook. You get fit by *doing*!

When you put these concepts into practice, it is necessary to instill in your sales force the lesson it doesn't matter if they win the next contract or make the next sale. Even if they don't, they will be helping your company by practicing emotional intelligence. What looks like "failure" is, in fact, part of building a successful strategic sales culture.

Consider the all-too-common case of a customer reacting negatively to a salesperson. The customer might be rude and react angrily or huffily to even the most respectful and tactful sales pitch. How does the salesperson react? Well, they might meet that anger with anger. They might say something they regret. Is this ideal? No. Is it the end of the world? Also, no! By practicing emotional intelligence—even in moments of "failure" when we react with negative emotion—we become more emotionally intelligent, as described in this chapter.

As we have seen, building an emotionally intelligent sales culture can lead to business success. A sales culture focused on relationship building rather than the quick sale, and one that manages expectations with empathy, is one that will forge genuine relationships with customers beyond a single sales cycle or a single quarter. The key to strategic sales is emotion, remember. Your customers are buying a feeling, and a sales team that sees its client base as people, not just customers, is a team setting the stage for long-term success.

With deliberate practice and training to promote emotional intelligence in sales, your team will see the results. And your business will never be the same. By creating a new generation of thought leaders, your sales force will transform your company for the better, putting it on a glide path to growth and ensuring that prospective customers view your business as the go-to solution to many of their problems.

Chapter 6

Empathy—Competitive Advantage in Business

"Empathy is one of our greatest tools of business that is most underused."

—Daniel Lubetzky

"Respect, Integrity, Communication and Excellence." — have you heard of this phrase before? "We treat others as we would like to be treated ourselves. We do not tolerate abusive or disrespectful treatment. Ruthlessness, callousness, and arrogance don't belong here."

You might be surprised to learn that the above quotes were the motto and mission statement of Enron Corporation. Yes, *that* Enron. What can this teach us? Well, for starters, it shows that the actions of a company can fall far, far short of their stated ideals. The loftiest mission statements and the most stirring mottoes can create positive brand associations for your company, but they can't be internalized and reinforced by simply posting them in the offices. It is what you *do*, not what you *say,* that matters most in business — actions speak lauder the words.

The story of Enron is the story of a company that reached dramatic heights without embracing its values. As a result, it faced a dizzying fall. The ill-fated company's collapse affected thousands of employees and shook Wall Street to its core because of lies, fraud, callousness, and arrogance. Enron's shareholders lost $74 billion, leading to the company's bankruptcy in 2001. In time, "Enron" became shorthand for the century's biggest corporate deception and the notorious demise of a once-successful company.

Many said Enron as a business was a house of cards built on a pool of gasoline. People thought Enron fell because of the complicated nature of the financial transactions they were engaged in. But today, with the benefit of hindsight, we all can understand this isn't a story about why a particular business fell. It's about how people, in reality, behave. It was a human tragedy. Enron shows us the dark side of human behavior— how pride, greed, and deceit can ruin lives and fortunes. It's worth remembering that in power at Enron were former geeks. They were numbers of people who weren't too concerned with the big picture or how their actions affected others, let alone the entire country and economy. They didn't ask themselves, "What are we doing?" Or "How will my actions help or harm Enron's stakeholders, customers, and employees?" A collection of quotes from past Enron employees who don't want to reveal their identity show several important questions they didn't ask:

"I didn't ask myself why…"
"I didn't ask my colleague why…"
"I didn't ask my manager why enough."
"I didn't ask my employer why enough."

These former Enron employees all agreed that you can gain the entire world, all the trinkets and all the trophies in the world, the corner office and all the perks that come with it—you can gain all this and still lose your soul.

Although the seven-sentence suicide note of former Enron's vice-chairman J. Clifford Baxter reveals little about whether his former employer's collapse may have moved him to take his life, it does show the anguish of a disconsolate person. When Baxter's handwritten note was released, it was published in many national and local newspapers. As Chicago Tribute published, it read - "*I am so sorry for this. I feel I just can't go on. I've always tried to do the right thing, but where there was once immense pride, now it's gone,*" *Baxter, 43, wrote to his wife, Carol, in block letter.* "*I love you and the children so much. I just can't be any good to you or myself. The pain is overwhelming. Please try to forgive me. Cliff.*"

I am sorry this sounds very disturbing. And Enron was an extreme case, but it reveals something eternal about business: not recognizing others' feelings is tremendously costly for an organization, its employees, customers, and stakeholders. When business leaders behave thoughtlessly toward others, they lower the entire organization's Emotional Intelligence. A manager needs to know how others feel to manage employees, satisfy stakeholders, deal with customers, and lead through changes. Emotionally intelligent business leaders are the ones best equipped to tackle today's most difficult workplace problems.

Stress and Disengagement at Work

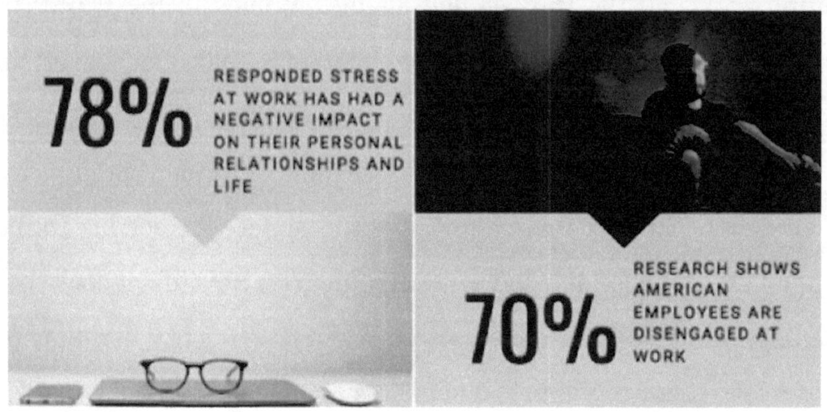

Korn Ferry, a research firm specializing in executive assessments, emphasizing leadership style and potential, surveyed about 2,000 professionals. The results should surprise none of us: 76 percent of respondents said stress at work had had a negative impact on their relationships and life. As more employees shift to remote work, the boundary between personal and business lives is shrinking.

Empathy is the tool you can use to solve these problems faced by your workforce. Not only that, but empathy is also an important and necessary component of customer service that allows you to connect with customers. In a 2016 study of 150 CEOs, over 80 percent of them identified empathy as the key to success. These numbers have not changed in the last four years. Today, 92 percent of CEOs claim that their organization is empathetic.

Stepping into empathy also allows us to stand in our integrity and connect with our counterpart at the same time. In today's information age, where information is an intangible and invisible aspect of a business, some scholars call this "invisible age". With invisible technologies, invisible hierarchies, invisible offices, and even invisible money moving around, a strong set of integrity in business has become more crucial than ever before.

I want to show you how empathy can help you be a better business leader.

The Most Significant Competitive Advantage in a Business

If you're not already convinced that empathy can strengthen your business, I want to show you why I believe this. What follows are some of the most visible benefits of fostering an empathetic workplace.

Improved employee engagement and productivity.

Now consider the employee side. Many of us have experience with workplaces where the entire staff is stressed, fearful, and disengaged. (If you haven't, consider yourself lucky!) Why would employees feel this way? A lack of empathy in the workplace. Leaders and managers who bring empathy into the workplace can make employees' lives better. Employees who feel better at work will be more engaged in their work and more productive.

The best tool for customer service and retention.

Suppose you bought a smartphone that immediately broke. If you called the manufacturer's customer service department, and they listened to your problems and developed a solution tailored to your needs, you would feel good about that company, wouldn't you? Empathy is the way to engender these feelings of goodwill among your customers. A happy customer feels like you understand their concerns and will work hard to address them. To keep your customers coming back, there's no better tool than empathy.

Better stakeholder engagement and collaboration.

The same is true for any other stakeholders involved in your business. If contractors or suppliers sense that your workplace is empathetic, they will respond in kind. Friction will be reduced, and these stakeholders will work hard to deliver for you.

Increased sales, loyalty, and referrals.

You wouldn't buy a car from a salesperson who laughed at the vehicle you drove onto the lot, mocked your taste in cars, and dismissed your questions about safety features, would you? Of course not! So why would any customer want to deal with a business that refused to treat them with empathy? Employing empathy in the business world is an effortless way to build goodwill with your clients and prospective customers. Do you want to increase sales? Do you want your customers to be loyal to your brand? Do you want them to refer your business to other customers? If so, try being empathetic when you're interacting with them.

Greater competitive advantage and market value.

This translates to a stronger, more robust business. Loyal customers, engaged stakeholders, and productive workers will give you a competitive advantage and ultimately raise your market value.

Empathy in Emotional Intelligence

We now know that empathy is an important business skill but let's break down the concept to understand what it is and how to instill it in your workplace. Let's start with the basics of interpersonal communication. The first step toward skillful social behavior is social knowledge or awareness. This awareness or ability to tune in to others and feel what they are feeling is called empathy. Without empathy, we have difficulty sustaining relationships in our personal lives or business. People with sound Emotional Intelligence have the ability to maintain good relationships in all areas of their lives.

Empathy is one of the cornerstones of Emotional Intelligence. It refers to the ability not only to understand another person's emotions and perspective but also to respond so it demonstrates understanding. This demonstration of understanding is the basis of effective communication and the foundation for trust and connection. In her book *The Role of Empathy in Emotional Intelligence*, Emily Sterrett writes: **When someone starts to tell us about their situation, our limbic brain instantly searches its storehouse of memories for a time when we had a similar experience and felt the same way.** Feeling it internally is just a start; we must also try to label the feeling. The basic language of emotion works not only to describe our own emotions but also to offer us the language for empathy.

Indeed, labeling the emotions for anyone you interact or work with requires using all your experience, knowledge, and perception of Emotional Intelligence. In business, as in any other realm of life, we summon all of our past experiences and emotions when confronting a new situation. Empathy requires not just talking but listening and trying to understand what another person is feeling. Do they feel regretful, neglected, demoralized, guilty? Do they feel on edge or nervous? If you notice, and if you can identify what someone is feeling, you can express empathy by acknowledging how they may be feeling. This gives the signal to people you are tuned into their feelings and emotions. For example, a coworker who is nervous before giving a big presentation will feel seen, understood, and put at ease if you tell them, "I know how you're feeling. Presentations are always difficult, but it's OK to be nervous. You'll do great.

Harness Empathy into a tool for your Business

In this chapter, I am going to provide you with tips to help you harness your empathy into a tool that can help you. You can apply these insights to become a better negotiator, a more aware supervisor, and a sound decision-maker. I want to break down three types of empathy that can help you in leadership and business: Cognitive Empathy, Tactical Empathy, and Compassionate Empathy.

Cognitive Empathy in Business

Cognitive empathy differs from "emotional empathy" (we will review this later in this chapter), which happens when you literally feel the other person's emotions alongside them. Daniel Goleman, renowned psychologist, and author of the 1995 book *Emotional Intelligence* defined cognitive empathy as "Simply knowing how the other person feels and what they might be thinking—sometimes called perspective-taking."

This is an extremely useful skill in leadership and negotiations. As you get to know your employees or stakeholders socially and not just professionally, you will better understand what they are feeling. That does not mean you have to agree with everything they are thinking or feeling, of course; it just allows you to see things from their perspective. Empathy builds trust in the workplace.

As I became more curious about empathy and how it can be a competitive advantage in business, I found myself thinking about great actors. Truly gifted actors don't just fake feelings. I believe genuinely great actors are the ones who can find the emotional truth in a scene, channel that feeling, and then deliver it in front of the camera. They have the ability to immerse themselves in the role fully they're playing and not just communicate the emotions the character is feeling. I have had the good fortune to get to know a few actors whom I respect deeply. I interviewed the actor, producer, director, and writer Melody Brooke recently, and I was curious to know what she thought about the role of empathy in acting. When I asked how her experience as an actor relates to developing genuine empathy, she flipped my question back to me. She said that in any work environment, each of us is given a "role," and each of us should try to play the role to the best of our ability, just like an actor. The better an actor is—and, by extension, the better anyone is at the "role" that they are called to play—the more they can develop the ability to connect to others genuinely. Brooke told me that that's what a true actor does:

they put themselves in the character's shoes to understand their feelings. Brooke is also a life coach, and she reminded me that it's imperative for leaders not to get "consumed" by empathy. In the "roles" we play at work, we have to do our best to connect with our coworkers genuinely, but we shouldn't be overwhelmed by the energy and emotions of others. Instead, our job is to understand what others are feeling so we can empower them to tackle problems and create solutions.

In the workplace, leaders should try to embrace the "roles" they are given. Understanding the feelings of those around you can equip you to interact with your them more effectively. As you get better at channeling your empathy to benefit your business, your next step should be instilling a culture of empathy that your employees and the people you manage can draw on to become more empathetic themselves.

It may not always be possible to hire the most empathetic people, but the good news is empathy can be developed or improved in the workplace. Here are a few ways to develop empathy at work:

Believe that people have good intentions.

Rule number one: If you have hired a candidate, go with the assumption they have the best of intentions. If they have negative intentions, they will change their behavior when they encounter coworkers who have adapted to the culture of empathy you have created.

Don't leave your most difficult employees behind.

Not everyone is at the same level. Don't leave your most challenging employees behind. Have an honest conversation with them. By taking time to understand their perspective, you can understand their situation better—and you'll set a positive example of empathy in action.

Develop genuine curiosity in your staff.

This might sound strange when applied to the American workplace, but I have found this a useful tool at many workplaces around the world (including some workplaces in the US, as well). Develop a genuine attitude of curiosity and interest in others' emotions. Try to make a mental note about what feelings someone is likely to have in certain situations. When you ask them how they are, and their answers don't quite tally with how they sound (the emotional cues they're communicating), ask them if everything is all right. The more we can determine what another person's needs are by watching and by asking, the more able we will be to help them. The more help we provide, the better ally and coworker they will be.

Look for nonverbal cues.

It's not always what people say, but how they say it. Nonverbal cues refer to methods of communication not involving words—like body language and facial expressions. This is why it's so important to actually listen and not talk over people: if you're not paying close attention, it's easy to miss the emotional content communicated nonverbally. Observe your employees' or customers' nonverbal behavior carefully. Their tone of voice pauses in speech, increased or decreased intensity of speech, and their posture and facial expression, can tell you volumes. If you are paying attention, you can pick up more than half of the non-verbal communication, even on the phone. Most (about 90 percent) of a message is contained in nonverbal cues, while only about 10 percent of the meaning is included in the words we communicate.

Reflect on your experiences.

While you are talking to your employee or coworker and you identify a phrase that indicates the emotion another person is trying to show, reflect on an experience you've had that produced a similar emotion in you. How exactly did you feel? What were your physical sensations? Try to put an emotional label on this, and then let the other person know you've experienced that emotion, too. Nothing relays empathy better than this.

Reframe overgeneralizations to eliminate your personal biases and prejudices.

Reframing is a process where you identify negative or unhelpful thoughts and replace them with positive and empowering ones. It's a powerful way of changing the way you view a situation or person. Do not overgeneralize or allow yourself to engage in thinking like "He always…" or "She never…" Try replacing those thoughts with "They can do better if…" This is an effortless way to increase your empathy in everyday interactions.

As we'll see later in this book, sometimes it is wise to withhold empathy in business strategically. But as we have seen, there is a compelling case for embracing a culture of empathy in your business.

Tactical Empathy in Business

Chris Voss, a former FBI hostage negotiator and co-author of the bestseller *Never Split the Difference*, coined the term "tactical empathy" to describe the process of trying to understand your opponent on an emotional level to get a handle on challenging situations. Voss defines tactical empathy as "the deliberate influencing of your negotiating counterpart's emotions for the ultimate purpose of building trust-based influence and securing deals."

While his story pertains to hostage negotiation, the lessons he imparts also apply to the business world. Voss explains how to demonstrate to your counterpart you see the nuances of their emotions. The ways you modulate your voice, mirror the nonverbal cues and use "dynamic silence" all contribute to tactical empathy.

Tactical empathy is an incredibly valuable skill when it comes to negotiation. Consider these ways that it can help you when you're trying to sway your counterpart during a difficult negotiation:

Knowing what the other side wants.

If you can get a good understanding of what is essential to the other side—what they are concerned about and what they are attached to—it is much easier to find a way to work things out collaboratively. Building rapport and gaining trust by demonstrating that you understand the other person's priorities means using emotional intelligence to get what you want. This technique is used widely in customer service. When a customer comes to a well-trained support team with a problem, a good customer service agent first tries to ease the customer's concerns by asking questions, understanding the source of the tension, and empathizing with the customer.

Understanding the emotions driving the other party.

In any negotiation, you might use the common technique of making your case by presenting data, facts, and reasons. While this is a tried-and-true technique in the legal and business worlds, you might find this method doesn't always work, particularly in negotiations in which emotions are running high. A far more effective strategy is to use emotional intelligence to understand what your counterpart is feeling. Demonstrating that you understand the emotions that drive their decision-making will make you a much more effective negotiator.

It is using mirroring techniques in the workplace and sales.

Mirroring is a technique that can work well in any workplace, sales situation, or interpersonal relationships. With mirroring, one person adopts the physical and verbal behaviors of the other. This helps build rapport and agreement during the conversation. Mirroring generally works best during two-way conversations rather than in meetings or sales presentations that may involve only one-way communication with other people.

Using labeling techniques to gain confidence and get what you want.

Labeling the behavior of your counterpart can help you gain their trust and subtly influence their actions. Consider these applications:

a) If you want your counterpart in a negotiation to act a certain way, labeling allows you to nudge their behavior in the desired direction. For example, if you want your counterpart to be more collaborative, you might say, "I appreciate the way you're coming to the table to work through these issues with me." **Here, you're using positive reinforcement to get the person to continue showing behavior you find beneficial.** This applies beyond negotiation. If you want an employee to take on specific responsibilities, you can label them subtly when you see the employee even attempting to deal with that responsibility. You might say, "Great job asking for help!" or "I appreciated the way you came together with your team to meet the deadline." Showing appreciation for the slightest gesture will build trust and help the employee feel more self-confident. This is a common technique in parenting as well when we label our kids if we expect them to behave in specific ways. Don't we?

b) The second use of labeling involves giving a name to the other party's emotions during the conversation. For example, if a conversation feels tense, you might say, "I think this conversation is causing us both some stress, but I know we can work through it." In doing so, you release some of that tension and effectively tell your counterpart that you're in this together.

Leveraging verbal and nonverbal communication effectively.

If you have interviewed candidates for a job, you might have noticed how you pay attention to both verbal and nonverbal aspects of speech, such as - tone of voice, silences, pacing. It's interesting how easy it is to forget to pay attention to the nonverbal elements when involved in a conversation and negotiation. Using tone of voice and body language are essential aspects of tactical empathy. Former FBI negotiator Chris Voss explains the importance of modulating the tone of voice. Sometimes an assertive voice is less effective than the easy tone of a late-night DJ or the playful voice of an accommodator.

Tactical Empathy in Email Communication

When it comes to applying tactical empathy to negotiations, it's ideal to have in-person or phone conversations. But the reality is that, in the digital age, much communication is conducted online, through emails. Fortunately, the tools of tactical empathy can be applied to email communication.

When writing a follow-up email after an in-person or phone conversation, always try to summarize what you discussed. It need not have an exhaustive list of the details of the conversation, but it should include the outcome of the conversation. For example, if you receive an email confirming an agreement reached over the phone, you might respond, "Am I incorrect in assuming that we've agreed to X?" This way, you're forming a bond with your counterpart by establishing a shared agreement that the two of you reached together. If there isn't a specific outcome to a conversation, you might write, "I enjoyed our conversation. To summarize, here are the topics we talked about." Also set a date to follow up: "I would like to follow up on these two points on X date."

Email can support and amplify verbal communication efforts. Just because it's harder to read the other person's emotions in email, it is possible to apply tactical empathy to make written communication more connective. Consider these tips in email writing:

You don't have to respond to certain emails immediately.

If you receive an emotionally charged message, resist the urge to type out your gut reaction. Instead, come back to it when your negotiation skills aren't being overridden by emotion. Sleep on it.

One of Voss's rules is "Not more than five lines."[7]

Recognize that the person receiving the email probably has a lot on their plate; you don't want to add to their work by writing a long email. Voss also takes a lesson from virtual chess. Would you put all your moves in one email? No, you would parcel out valuable information, so the counterpart has the bandwidth to respond calmly.

Use softening the language to set the right tone.

If you are relaying a message that the recipient might find

---

[7] Former FBI negotiator Chris Voss

upsetting, insert as many "I'm sorry" and "I'm afraid" as possible. Likewise, if you assign someone a tedious task, instead of asking them to complete that task in a specific timeframe, you may write something like, "I'm sorry to drop this on you this week. I know this is a lot, but I hope you'll be able to get it to me by X date." Changing the tone of your message makes the content easier to swallow.

Read emails out loud before you send them.

This might sound obvious, but it never hurts to read out loud before sending important emails. This will tell you a lot about the emotional content of your message, and you might find you need to be more personable to put the recipient at ease.

Tell the truth but tell it positively.

Sometimes it's necessary to provide gentle criticism over email. While this is unavoidable, you can soften the blow by positively framing the change you'd like to see. For example, you might write, "The reason I am sending this email is that I want a win-win situation, and I think we can do this if we work collaboratively." Also, add this positive framing at the end of the message because the last impression is the lasting impression.

Choose subject lines and signoffs mindfully.

It can be easy to forget to review subject lines and signoffs before hitting "send," but it's important to think carefully about these aspects of email communication. Subject lines should be informative and never vague, and they should avoid language that might startle the recipient. Subject lines like "We need to talk..." sound ominous, so avoid these formulations. Finally, signoffs should be professional but warm, and they should communicate some aspect of your personality that the recipient would pick up on if you were talking in person.

Compassionate Empathy in Business

So far, we reviewed two primary forms of empathy that can be applied in business and leadership: cognitive empathy and tactical empathy. The third type of empathy I want to discuss is compassionate empathy, which involves feeling someone's pain and taking action to help. This is consistent with what we usually understand by compassion. Like sympathy, compassion is about feeling concern for someone, but with an additional move towards action to mitigate the problem. **Sometimes our counterparts need us to understand and sympathize with what they are going through and, crucially, help them take action to resolve the problem.**

My uncle was suffering from pneumonia in year 2016 with other complication. After spending days in the emergency and ICU, as he recovered enough to be brought home. Unfortunately, his condition relapse and he was brought to the emergency room once again. Due to complications caused by his recent illness, his condition wasn't improving. When the doctors realized he wasn't regaining consciousness, they quickly moved him to the ICU.

As soon as I heard the news, I flew to see him at the Harris Health Ben Taub Hospital in Houston. His condition became even more complicated; hospital staff had to keep him on the ventilator for two days. Unfortunately, my uncle didn't make it.

When the doctor entered the room, he understood the pain we were in, but he knew he had to deliver the news clearly. He looked us in the eye and told us what we feared: "He is actively dying, and there is no chance for survival." My aunt, their son (my cousin), and I were devastated.

The doctor paused so we could process this terrible news. After we had a chance to let this sink in, he continued. His tone was firm but calm, and we could sense he was aware of how difficult this would be for us to take in. "We worked tirelessly to see if there was even the slightest chance of saving him. So, when you ask, I can look into your eyes and say, 'We tried everything we could to save him.'"

I can't deny it: this was a tough moment for all of us. But I am grateful this doctor showed real compassionate empathy. He felt our pain, he considered how his words would affect us, and he delivered a message that eased some of our pain.

Although this is a personal story, you can relate even in business sometimes we need to relay favorable and unpleasant news to our counterparts. As you can see, empathy and compassion are about being genuine, not about pretending. You can't fake compassionate empathy. To communicate compassionately, you need to identify what another person is feeling, put yourself in their shoes, and feel their emotions alongside them. Only then can you offer them the help that will make them feel better.

Measuring Managers Empathy in Workplace

Well, if this is not just a touchy-feely topic, how can you measure this in your workplace? How can you perform a hetero evaluation of empathy and measure how the team members perceive their manager's empathy? You have two ways to measure. Team members in a group can assess what they feel about working in the company and for the manager. Second, the team can assess how their manager would self-assess their own empathy. I did some research and found there are some standard tools available for this assessment. Notable among them are, the Interpersonal Reactivity Index (Davis, 1980) and the Empathy Quotient (Baron-Cohen and Wheelwright, 2004).

For simplicity, the questionnaire for measuring empathy for managers and leaders by their subordinates can include these –

What do you feel about working in this company?

What do you feel about working with your manager?

How satisfied you are in your job?

Do you feel like your managers listen to you?

Does your manager encourage to talk about what you feel?

You might have seen similar questionnaires before. Such employee surveys serve as the barometers of the emotional health of the business and will keep you connected with the people you care about.

Emotional Empathy Can be Good and Bad in Business

When we hear the word "empathy," we tend to first think about emotions. We can call this "emotional empathy." Emotional empathy can be good and bad in the business world. When we experience emotional empathy, we understand and feel others' emotions psychologically and even bodily. This comes in handy for some service professionals, such as doctors, nurses, care providers, and social workers. Emotional empathy allows them to connect with the people they're caring for. Emotional empathy provides a shortcut to retrieving information about the person based on similar reactions they've seen in the past. For example, a nurse administering a vaccine will find it easy to sense when a patient is nervous, and they can use that information to set the patient at ease.

However, in many areas of business, emotional empathy can sometimes be a detriment. You may become overwhelmed by the emotions you're sensing in others. As a result, you may be unable to make an unbiased, sound decision.

When to Reject Empathy in Business

Sometimes, though, empathy might not be the most appropriate tool to use. In a contentious work relationship, showing your empathy can get in your goal of influencing mindset. Linguist Bilyana Martinovski has studied the role of empathy in negotiation, and she found that being empathetic doesn't consistently smooth over differences. Similarly, if the person you're speaking with offers empathy, it is sometimes appropriate to "reject" the display of empathy politely and press your demand. A good example of when to reject empathy is when a fundamental disagreement is getting in the way of the organization's operations or if negotiation is stalled.

Martinovski gives the example of a doctor negotiating with an Army captain who is holding up much-needed medical supplies. The doctor, frustrated, acknowledges but rejects the captain's show of empathy. What this demonstrates is that accepting--or giving--empathy is sometimes an inappropriate response. Rejecting empathy is occasionally precisely what is required to influence someone to take your concerns to heart. Sometimes, a person's display of empathy might be insincere or simply a technique to allay your legitimate concerns.

The Science Behind Empathy

When I read studies about the business world, I'm always curious about the hard science that supports the researchers' findings. And when it comes to the science of empathy and compassion, the results are incredibly fascinating.

Mirror neurons are a subcategory of motor-command neurons—the parts of our brain activated when we move our hands or pick up an object. Neuroscientists Vilayanur S. Ramachandran and William Hirstein, in their 1998 paper "The Perception of Phantom Limbs," describe how mirror neurons work. The results, as Ramachandran said in an interview, made him "jump out of his seat." Ramachandran explains how mirroring behavior works in our brains: When you pick up a cup of coffee, your mirror neurons direct the sequence of muscular movements required to complete this commonplace but neurologically complex task. Over the last ten years, researchers have discovered these mirror neurons fire not only when you pick up a cup but also when you watch someone executing the same action.

That's right. When you see someone picking up a cup, your mirror neurons fire as though you yourself are doing this action. In other words, mirror neurons are mind-reading neurons. They create a virtual-reality simulation of another person's mind, and they form the basis of empathizing with another person.

According to an article published by the NIH, Ramachandran and Diane Rogers-Ramachandran created the famous "mirror" or "virtual reality box therapy." This device was constructed by placing a mirror vertically in a wooden box. They worked with one-armed patients who experienced the sensation of a "phantom limb" — it is a sensation that an amputated or missing limb is still attached. The patient would put their healthy arm into one side and the phantom limb into the other. The top and front sides of the box were open, which allowed the patient to look into the box, but for the treatment, they had to cock their head to one side such that they could see the mirror from the side of the box with the healthy arm. Next, they were asked to move their healthy arm around until their mirror image "superimposed the felt position of the phantom." If working correctly, when patients performed "mirror-symmetrical movements," they would see their phantom arm "resurrected."

Phantom Limbs: The Mirror Box[8]

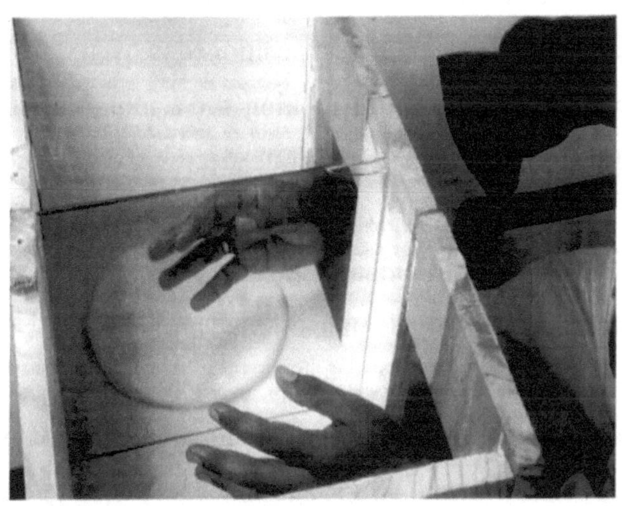

A major application of this breakthrough research addresses an interesting clinical problem: how do you treat a missing body part? Many patients who have lost body parts manage with painkillers or hypnotism, but for some, nothing works. That's what's so revolutionary about the mirror box method. Our mirror neurons are so powerful that they can treat genuine pain that even strong painkillers can't lessen. If you search "Phantom Pain Mirror Box" videos on the internet, you will see how many patients use this to manage such pain.

This is the power of tactical mirroring and empathy. If they can help a patient with their pain who have lost body parts, think about what they can do for your dissatisfied customers and depressed employees.

---

[8] Published in NIH — V.S. Ramachandran's mirror box. V.S. Ramachandran and William Hirstein, 'The Perception of Phantom Limbs: The D.O. Hebb Lecture', Brain, 121 (1998), 1603–630: 1621.

The stakes couldn't be higher: in today's fast-changing business world, businesses with a culture based on empathy, compassion, and understanding will be the ones best positioned to overcome challenges and achieve success. If you're looking for a tool that can increase customer loyalty, lead to more referrals, decrease employee turnover, and increase the productivity of your workforce, look no further than empathy. By creating an empathetic workplace, you will give your business a competitive advantage *and* provide the basis for a flourishing of innovation. Ultimately, business leaders have the responsibility of instituting a culture of empathy. And that starts with "the person in the mirror." CEOs and managers need to demonstrate the empathy they want to see reflected in the employees, customers, and business partners.

Chapter 7

Leading Changes with Emotional Intelligence

"The first step toward change is awareness. The second step is acceptance."

—Nathaniel Branden

We have seen how important emotional intelligence is in the business world. It can ignite motivation, lead to improved group performance, and confer a competitive advantage among many others. It should come as no surprise, then, that emotional intelligence can be applied to one of the most difficult challenges any business faces— confronting changes. Leaders with emotional intelligence are equipped to lead their organizations through tough changes. And in today's economy, emotionally intelligent leadership can lead the changes more gracefully.

That's because the world is changing—and it is changing quickly.

Recent technological improvements, including digitization, an adaptation of AI, and mobile technologies, have increased the speed of social and economic changes and nowhere is this more evident than in the business world.

Think, for example, about something as seemingly simple as the "office". The concept of office has changed so quickly over the past decade it can be hard to even define what we mean by an office. In the early 2010s, many businesses moved from siloed cubicles to open-floor plans that facilitate communication. Then, just as quickly, millions of workers found that their homes had to double as their offices due to the COVID-19 pandemic. Now, many companies continued to allow flexibility in work-from-home policies, which are enabled by technologies like video communications cloud platforms etc.

This example shows us we saw two giant paradigm shifts in a few short years. While this is undoubtedly an exciting time, it is also an uncertain one. Rank-and-file employees and CEOs alike are experiencing whiplash and wondering how they can adapt their businesses and themselves to emerging realities. When rapid changes like these happen, employees often resist those changes. It's human nature. We're afraid of changes that present unknowns, and uncertainties. People make plans based on their current situation, so when they hear about any major business change, they worry, anticipating that they'll suffer from the effects of changes. Their fear sometimes turns into anger and resentment, compels people to resist change.

But there is always change on the horizon, whether you recognize it or not. And that's why honing your ability to adapt to change is so important. Many businesses and business models have a life of themselves, and they can go on using the old playbook even as the world changes right in front of them. If the business doesn't change with the world, though, they can pay a price.

The Importance of Embracing Changes

Many retail companies were impacted amid the rapid changes of the e-commerce era. From the end of World War II into the 1970s, Sears sales were at an all-time high. According to the *New York Times*, the retailer had over 350,000 employees in its ranks and was able to provide many a clear path to the middle-class. Sears should have kept its eyes open and developed initiatives to adapt to changes amid rapidly shifting consumer behavior changes. Consumers were getting accustomed to online and mobile experiences. Sears' inability to deliver on these omnichannel experiences is just one of the many factors that led to the downfall of the retail giant. Sears' failure to innovate derived from an inability to change its psychology and a failure to adapt to digital transformation.

Consider the infamous case of Blockbuster. The video-rental chain once owned over 9,000 retail stores in the United States. But as streaming emerged, Blockbuster lost their customers. Why? Because of the greatest form of executive negligence — fear of change. Their fear of change spilled over into many business decisions they made, preventing them from acting early and competently pivoting to streaming. In 2010 Blockbuster filed for bankruptcy because it failed to keep up with competitors like Netflix, which created a DVD-by-mail service. What happened in the video streaming industry after that is history. And so is Blockbuster.

These are just a couple of examples of the organizations resisting changes, you may know several of them and some you may know even firsthand. So how can you avoid the sad story of Sears's downfall and a Blockbuster-sized failure? Embrace the right change swiftly.

Looking into The Future

Fortunately, in many areas you actually do, in a sense have a crystal ball that lets you look at least five years in the future. That crystal may be in the area driven by innovation, such as - technology, R&D, healthcare, supply chains, and manufacturing. Innovations we see today were baked years ago to meet the needs of the future. When we look at technologically advanced fields like these, we can see where the world is heading. I am often surprised that some businesses don't look closely enough at technology to glimpse what is going to happen in the near future. Nothing, after all, is abrupt in technology: it shows the shape of the future, in the here and now. Look at any technology-driven changes around you to see the future.

Think of it this way: technology is built for the future. The technology available for use in this quarter was created years ago. Whenever Apple brings a new piece of technology to the market, they're rolling out what their team set in motion several quarters (or years) ago. The same is true for the other technologies we hear so much about, from 5G and AI to blockchain. In a very real sense, then, we have seen the future!

The future is there for everyone to see if they have the resources, time, and vision to look for it. While it's true that the future is not evenly distributed—not all people have the same access to information related to technological changes—business leaders like those at Blockbuster or Sears certainly had access to this glimpse into the future. Unfortunately for them - they chose not to look.

One of the reasons so many business leaders don't see what's right in front of them is that they don't want to admit that the world is changing. Even though technological changes are clear as day, some leaders choose to hide their heads in the sand and deny the inevitable. This is understandable—and it's also avoidable.

Leading through Changes

The first step to embrace change is to admit that you fear change. While this sounds obvious, many of us have a blind spot when it comes to our own appetite for change. Consider a scenario Spencer Johnson relates in his world-famous book *Who Moved My Cheese?* Johnson describes a business leader who asks a roomful of employees, "How many of you are afraid of change?" Only one hand went up. The leader continued, "How many of you think other people are afraid of change?" The entire roomful of people raised their hands.

What does that tell us? One of two things is clear: many of us are either in denial, or we're not even aware that we're afraid of change. This is not meant to shame people for fearing change. Rather, I want us all to be honest about the negative emotions we have when it comes to change so we can move beyond them and embrace change.

If you are a business leader, the change has to start with you. After that, you can focus on corporate change efforts, such as reengineering, quality management, restructuring, and implementing cultural changes.

Conscious-change leadership calls for and is fueled by greater emotional self-awareness. Initiative-taking and deliberate leaders are more conscious and aware of the subtle dynamics of transformation, especially regarding people and processes. They are not only conscious about it but also develop a strategy to deal with it and prepare their team for evolution. True leaders perceive human elements as well as the nuances of change processes.

Now that we have established the necessity of embracing change and keeping sight of the human element of change processes, I want to outline several actionable tips on effectively leading through changes:

Communicate a sense of sound vision and direction.

Stakeholders and employees will be willing to cooperate with the changes only if they know that the change is possible. Otherwise, they will doubt that change will occur, and they'll cling to the current ways of thinking and operating. Use all the possible communication channels to share your vision: emails, newsletters, management meetings, and all-hands meetings.

Walk the talk and lead by example.

If you want your team to embrace change, you must become a living example of what you want to see in them. Nothing undermines a team's appetite for change more than leaders who say one thing and do another. When you lead by example, you create a picture of what's possible with the changes.

Establish a sense of urgency.

People throughout the organization must understand that business, as usual, is the surest path to the business's obsolescence. Communicating the vital necessity of change is key.

Motivate all the stakeholders.

Business change requires aggressive cooperation from others. But getting everyone to cooperate requires motivation. Without the right motivation, stakeholders will not cooperate, which may undermine the change efforts.

Help ease people out of their comfort zones.

Change leads to discomfort, as we've seen. And embracing that discomfort is the best way to help people throughout the organization accept change. Understand that people will be hesitant to embrace changes and help ease them into the new way of operating.

Create thought leaders.

Developing talent that shares your passion is a terrific way to promote change throughout the business. Many organizations have too many managers and not enough leaders. Empower your employees to take the torch and lead their coworkers through the change process.

Let people fail.

Failure is an influential teacher, as it can show people the consequences of not embracing change. Letting your people fail can be an effective tool of development, as long as you, the leader, properly coach them through it. However, I advise great caution while using this tactic. But done strategically, failure can contribute to a resilient workforce, as I have described in the next chapter.

Remove obstacles.

Any time we have to make a change, in business or in any other area of life, we face challenges. Leaders always face obstacles to the changes they're proposing, some of which are organizational and others that are personal in nature. There are always skeptics and doubters who don't think the business can do it. There are those who say, "We don't have the time or budget to do this" or "This is going to create more work for us." Others may say, "We don't have the skills to do it," and still others will lack motivation. A great leader will recognize and remove these obstacles. Emotional intelligence is the key to doing so: let your team know you understand these doubts and explain to employees how the changes will save time and make work easier. Meet your employees where they are, emotionally speaking, and help them understand that they can overcome obstacles.

Create short-term wins.

We live in a world where the majority of people are used to expecting instant gratification. Major change may take a longer time to bear fruit, though, so it's important to let people enjoy the little wins along the way. Encourage "small sprints" by breaking down challenges into their most logical components and assigning the pieces to task-centered teams to solve. This way, your team will experience the gratification of completing tasks. Consider using small groups and creating ideas in rapid cycles that allow teams to work together and stay connected to the higher purpose of the project of changing the organization.

Reward people.

Everyone involved in the change process should be celebrated, and your employees need rewards during the process. Be careful, though, to keep focused on the long-term and don't pop the champagne until all the work is done.

I encourage you to follow these ten pieces of advice. Why? Because change is hard, and many organizations don't respond well to it. **According to research by McKinsey, about 70 percent of all changes in organizations fail.** This is an astounding statistic that reflects just how difficult it can be to implement change. Failed transformations share common problems. McKinsey's senior partner Harry Robinson explains how McKinsey removes self-defeating behaviors and attitudes before they derail the change process. It is necessary to put the right change-management structure in place and hold regular performance-management discussions to track the success of the implemented changes.

Managing People-centric Organizational Changes

Perhaps the most challenging and daunting problem leaders have to account for in implementing people-centric organizational changes. This is an emotional process for people throughout an organization. It can generate multiple psychological responses, affecting your and your team's ability to understand, navigate, and embrace the unknown new realities that are forthcoming. Facing and handling the fear that employees feel can be mind-numbing for managers. Some may fear that the change initiative will fail and result in harmful consequences. Others may be more fearful of changes required if the initiative is successful; it might change their day-to-day jobs or their role within the company. To counter the fear that employees will bring to this process, leadership should frame change in terms of what can be gained, rather than what will be lost. Highlighting what each stakeholder will gain from the initiative will motivate them to buy in and help make change happen. For a process so heavily influenced by the emotions of all involved, it is necessary for leadership to be emotionally intelligent.

To improve your self-awareness and management skills, reflect on these questions:

- What most concerns you about the change your business is implementing? Potential areas of concern could include employee skepticism or difficulty understanding the concerns of your team.

● How can you address these concerns effectively? Possible answers include active listening, strategic empathy, and constant communication with stakeholders.

● Who can support you during this process (or who needs support)? Support is a two-way street, and just as you need the help of other members of the leadership team, your employees need your help to navigate the emotional difficulties that come with change.

What we think becomes a reality. This means that if your team thinks change is impossible, they will be setting themselves up for failure. It is the responsibility of leadership to help the team through the proposed changes. This starts with being emotionally intelligent enough to recognize what your employees are feeling. Wise leaders recognize and monitor subtle cues that communicate hesitancy, anxiety, and fear. By anticipating that your team will experience these emotions, you can be prepared to adapt in the moment to address and allay their concerns.

By harnessing the power of emotional intelligence, you can help your employees embrace change. Life moves on, and so should we. Emotionally intelligent leadership can help all stakeholders let go and move on for the benefit of the business. It's important to note that some things shouldn't change—for example, your core values and your commitment to understanding the emotions of your team.

Emotional intelligence is the compass that can guide you through the emotional turbulence that comes with change.

As we have seen, change is the one constant in the world. History is littered with the unfortunate stories of once-successful businesses that failed because they failed to embrace change. Change doesn't mean that every company has to follow in the path of Sears or Blockbuster though. By embracing change and harnessing the power of emotional intelligence to lead your employees through the anxiety and fear that often accompany organizational change, you can ensure that your business can take advantage of, rather than suffer from, the rapid changes that are transforming the business world.

The key is to always strive to understand the emotions of your employees. By putting yourself in their shoes and really feeling the fear that they're experiencing, you will be better positioned to help them understand how the change will actually make their lives easier—and, in the process, position the business stronger.

One of the most difficult changes businesses face arises during mergers and acquisitions (M&A). In the next chapter, we will discuss in detail how to navigate through the changes emerging from M&As and how to manage emotions during that process.

Chapter 8

Managing Emotions in Mergers & Acquisitions

"Emotions cloud people's ability to compromise, to see that a lot of issues aren't personal but simply economic. You have to keep people focused on their common interests."

— Charles Mulaney Jr., M&A Attorney and Partner

For as often as high-profile mergers and acquisitions (M&As) make financial headlines, they are two of the most misunderstood terms in the business world. If you asked a common person what an M&A is, you'd likely hear some variation on the following: M&As involve the joining of two companies. That's not incorrect, but it also doesn't capture the core concept of M&A. As the two terms have become increasingly blended and used in conjunction with each other, many people in business have lost sight of the differences between mergers, on one hand, and acquisitions on the other.

So, what is the main difference between mergers and acquisitions?

To start with, a merger occurs when two business entities consolidate into a new organization with a single ownership and management structure. In contrast, an acquisition refers to the takeover of one entity by another.

Now, you might ask, why is this distinction important? Well, as it turns out, depending on the nature of the M&A—whether two businesses are merging or whether one business is taking over another—the aftermath of this seismic business decision can have enormous effects on your business, particularly when it comes to emotion in the workplace.

We might add to our definitions above an "emotional" distinction that sets mergers apart from acquisitions. The emotional connotation of a merger—which we might call "friendly"—differs greatly from that of an acquisition—which can have a "hostile" emotional connotation. Even these black-and-white distinctions break down, though, and the "friendliest" merger can often leave an ocean of emotional turmoil in its wake. After any M&A transaction, what C-level executives and consultants euphemistically call the "post-merger integration," if not managed effectively, can be a period of tribal conflict, uncertainty, and chaos caused by a leadership void.

Besides being highly complex organizational and legal events, M&As are highly *emotional* business events. Anyone who has experienced a merger, or an acquisition knows this. When a company's leadership structure and team change, and when "outsiders" join the company, some employees respond to these changes with vulnerability. They may become sullen, disengaged, and may start taking excessive sick leaves. Other employees show resilience and see opportunity in change. They are thrilled by the opportunity to work with new team members, and they're excited to see company policies change. Employees with negative responses show anxiety, confusion, selfishness, and blame, while other employees show courage, optimism, faith, and determination.

How your employees respond to an M&A is largely determined by your managerial behavior and communication styles. If there's anxiety, disagreement, and turmoil at the top of the leadership chart, these negative emotions will trickle down to the entire team. Similarly, if leaders demonstrate openness to change and uncertainty, they can influence their team to roll with the changes and embrace the good that comes with change.

When M&A Becomes Inevitable

Mergers and acquisitions are most common in technology, health care, financial services, and retail sectors. Here are the top four reasons why and when M&A becomes inevitable:

To sustain growth.

This applies primarily to mature companies looking to capture more market share by acquiring a competitor.

To cut costs.

Merging with a company that offers a similar service can reduce costs and liabilities by streamlining services.

For survival.

Acquiring a competitor is a way to eliminate future competition before it threatens your business.

To replace leadership.

When the owner of a company can't identify a successor for a leadership role, merging with another company provides access to fresh talent.

Additionally, when departments are merged within a company, and organizational charts are streamlined, we can think of this as a type of an integration. The business drivers and consolidation processes for internal group integration may differ from external M&As, but the emotional aspects and team dynamics are similar.

4 REASONS WHY AND WHEN M&A BECOME INEVITABLE

To Sustain Growth

When companies are in the mature phase of their life cycle, it becomes difficult for them to sustain the competitive marketplace's growth. Sometimes the only way to grow is to take market share from a competitor. This usually happens when companies are in the mature phase of their life cycle.

To Cut Cost

When companies' liabilities increase and profit decline, they pressure the market and board to cut costs. They start to seek companies that have similar products or services; combining can reduce costs. When companies merge, they can combine locations or reduce operating costs by integrating and streamlining support functions.

For Survival

Many companies use mergers and acquisitions to grow and survive. For example, to eradicate competition and to create market power. Such deals allow the acquirer to eliminate future competition and gain a larger market share. Very often mergers between companies that do not compete directly with each other but still affect competition negatively when merged.

Replace Leadership

This can be seen in a private company, not much in a public company. The company may need to merge or be acquired if the current owners can't identify someone within the company to succeed them. Although, this is not as common as other reasons for M&As.

Why Do Mergers & Acquisitions Fail

According to a research analysis by the *Harvard Business Review*, the failure rate for M&As sits between 70 to 90 percent. This is an astoundingly high figure. Most M&As fail to reach their initial goals, and they destroy the value of an organization. When you consider the technical and cultural factors that occur during the average merger or acquisition, this is not surprising. Why M&As fail is a topic of endless study. The root cause of M&A failure or success is directly related to the collective leadership capabilities of the acquirer and target companies. For the acquirer, the executive board identifies leaders to work on the implementation. For the target, the management identifies senior executives to retain for 1–3 years.

The chaos of this turnover often creates a lack of accountability and ownership, and customers get neglected. Stepping into this leadership void, competitors swoop in and skim off those customers. "The main beneficiaries of mergers in the computer industry have been competitors because companies become so focused on organizational matters that they lose sight of their customers," Ben Rosen, the chairman of Compaq, said about AT&T's acquisition of NCR in 1991.[9] According to Martinroll[10], a business and brand leadership organization, **"The reasons for failed mergers include tangible accounting and operation failures, but the most complex reasons deal with people, culture and human emotion. These are**

---

[9] 15 Simon London, "Inside Track: Risks of Grabbing a Tiger by the Tail," *Financial Times*, September 10, 2001.

[10] Martinroll - Business and Brand Leadership organization (Feb 2014)

also the most difficult to correct."

Fortunately, M&As need not lead to catastrophic failure for the parties involved. Avoiding these common pitfalls will help ensure that an M&A will be successful:

1. Negotiation Errors

It all begins with the negotiation. Complex deals like M&As require strategic analysis, communication, and leadership. When a company fails to assess the value of a target company and overpays the acquisition and advisory fees, this leads to financial failures.

Besides negotiating the financial terms, companies discussing an M&A deal need to account for culture as well. Leaders should do a cultural assessment to understand how these three **Ps** reflect tightness or looseness in both the companies: **People, Processes, and Practices.** Leaders on both sides should identify areas for compromise. "Tightly coupled" organizations (businesses with highly formal cultures) need to determine areas where they can embrace the informal, agile nature of "Loosely coupled" businesses, and vice versa. In tightly coupled organizations, supervisors know what their employees are doing, and management can coordinate cross-department efforts according to a centralized strategy. In loosely coupled organizations, employees have more autonomy, and different departments may operate without much coordination. There is no right or wrong way of managing an organization, and both structures have advantages and disadvantages. The important effort during M&As is for executives on both sides to identify areas for compromise so the companies can work together productively.

2. Fear and Greed

It's not just financial markets that are driven by fear and greed. Although companies may not publicly talk about it, many M&As are driven by fear and greed, too. Often, investors get caught up in a fever of greed, an excessive desire to grab a bigger piece of the pie. After all, it's human nature for most of us to want to acquire as much wealth as possible in the shortest time. But greed can lead to rash decision-making and a tendency to disregard the needs of others.

Just as an M&A deal can fall apart because of greed, the same can happen with fear, the unpleasant anticipation of liability, or vulnerability. When M&As are motivated by fear of rising costs, or lost revenue and profits, maybe it's not a good reason to merge.

3. Cultural Mismatches

Workplace culture is the personality of your organization. It's what makes your business unique, and it is the sum of your people's shared values, beliefs, behaviors, and attitudes. When two companies' workplace cultures are vastly different, or at odds with each other, it can make merging difficult, ultimately threatening the success of both parties. In a case study conducted by Isaac Dixon in the *Society for Human Resource Management*[11], culture was found to cause an astounding 30 percent of failed M&A integrations.

How can you avoid this if you're planning on an M&A? According to the management consulting firm Deloitte, when two

---

[11] Isaac Dixon, "Culture Management and Mergers and Acquisitions," Society for Human Resource Management, March 2005.

companies integrate, it is critical to develop a rigorous program with clearly stated objectives that address cultural integration. As Deloitte [12]points out, "Too often, culture is presented as a wooly and soft topic. When that happens, executives tend to slight the issue. This can generally be avoided by linking the cultural program to measurable business results."

The bottom line is, during an M&A, business leaders minimize culture at their own peril. Consider the case of Whole Foods. In June 2017, Whole Foods CEO John Mackey, who agreed to sell the company to Amazon, gushed that the partnership was "love at first sight." A year later, however, such optimism was hard to find in the company. Stories spread of employees literally crying on the job over Amazon's changes.

The two companies had concluded there was great value in capitalizing on each other's strengths. So, what went wrong? Whole Foods and Amazon failed to adequately account for their cultural compatibility—or lack thereof. Amazon's culture is tightly coupled. Rooted firmly in the manufacturing industry, Amazon has defined its processes to maximize efficiency. After speaking with current and former Amazon employees, the *New York Times* exposed a "bruising workplace" culture that is not for everyone, to put it lightly. To be the best "Amazonians" they can be, employees were encouraged to abide by 14 leadership principles inscribed on handy laminated cards.

Whole Foods, on the other hand, has a loosely coupled

---

[12] Deloitte Website: Leading through transition, Perspectives on the people side of M&A

organizational culture. Furthermore, high profit margin and rapid growth led to a culture of idealism. Creating the first certified "Organic National Supermarket" in the US provided Whole Foods' founders with considerable freedom in introducing unorthodox management methods that were foreign to the Amazon model.

While the merger might be viewed as a success in retrospect, it's worth considering "successful for whom?" It might be viewed as a win for Amazon, the acquiring company, but it seems likely that many Whole Foods employees viewed the acquisition differently. In determining whether an M&A is successful or not, we have to look at both the picture and the details. When we do that, we can see there can be losers even within otherwise "successful" M&As, and we must consider the employee morale of the acquired company.

There are myriads of other examples of M&A deals that did more harm than good because of cultural incompatibility: Alcatel and Lucent, New York Central and Pennsylvania Railroad, Quaker Oats, and Snapple, are just a few of the many companies that faced M&A complications due to culture.

4. Communication

Failure to adequately communicate during integration is another big cause of M&A failure. If employees don't know what the future holds—for the company and for their careers—they will feel left out of the loop, and their productivity will suffer. Immediately after a company announces their intention to engage in an M&A, many employees struggle to cope with stress and, as a result, resist the planned changes. They may feel insecure and fear that new leadership may view them as dispensable. Some employees will look for another job, leave the company, or—at the very least—become disengaged from their work.

Thus, an effective and timely communication plan can help manage these negative emotions during the M&A process. After a merger, projects and processes critical to a business can disintegrate, and low employee morale can ripple through the integration process. Ultimately, this can impact customer retention and potentially erode shareholder value. This is why it is so important to communicate clearly and effectively during the M&A process. A transparent M&A communication strategy can help manage negative emotions, build adaptive resilience, and make the new partnership successful.

If those in leadership, from the executive team to the management structure, demonstrate an inability to address their employees' concerns, group synergy will break down, swiftly leading to a toxic work environment. By the time this happens, the company will be well on its way to ensuring a downturn, if not the death of the organization. A. T. Kearney's Global PMI Survey[13] shows just how important communication is during an M&A. Factors such as delays in IT integration, the absence of a master plan, or a compromised organizational structure pale in comparison to anxiety about communication, with 58 percent of respondents listing this as a concern.

---

[13] A. T. Kearney's Global PMI Survey 1998/1999

Successful and Unsuccessful M&As

Let's look at some real-world examples of successful M&As. Consider the following high-profile M&As:

- **Disney and Pixar**: This merger gave Disney ownership of the world's most famous computer animation studio and its talent.

- **Exxon and Mobile**: The synergy benefits of this merger were greater and realized sooner than predicted.

- **Pfizer and Warner-Lambert**: This merger created the pharmaceutical industry's largest R&D budget.

- **Verizon and Vodafone**: This helped Verizon emerge as America's top broadband and telecom player.

- **AT&T and BellSouth**: Enabled faster and more economical deployment of next-generation IP networks.

- **Travelers Group and Citicorp**: Allowed Travelers to market mutual funds and insurance to Citicorp's retail customers.

Behind each of these successful M&A integrations was a thorough plan to merge distinct cultures and communicate clearly to head off employees' anxieties. What's striking is these are all established, well-known companies, and we might expect them to have the resources and know-how to pull off a tricky merger. Things become much more interesting when we look at a single company and explore how M&As can succeed in some cases and fail in others.

When Hewlett-Packard and Compaq announced an agreement to merge in 2001, it shocked the industry and sent shudders through the market. This was predicted to be a very painful and even disastrous integration. But in retrospect, this is now considered one of the most successful mergers in history, as they became an $87 billion global technology leader. How was this merger so successful? To begin with, HP and Compaq had a concrete vision and strategy for blending people and culture into one brand. Leaders were able to smoothly blend the two cultures because they had a lot in common. Carly Fiorina, CEO of HP at that time, showed great leadership in managing her company's culture. When she arrived at HP, she faced "the H-P Way," the almost sacrosanct culture of founders David Packard and Bill Hewlett. As she revealed, the culture at HP had become "a gentle bureaucracy of entitlement and consensus," and she sought to bring it back to its roots of valuing the individual, rewarding creativity, and focusing on great engineering. Compaq had a quite different corporate culture, but the merger was successful because leaders implemented a concrete strategy for blending the two cultures into one, taking the best aspects from each company.

Next, HP was aware of the difficulties of merging, and they were prepared to confront them. HP's head of human resources compared mergers to icebergs, where the real work takes place below the surface. The merger would produce one very large iceberg[14]—perhaps big enough to sink competitors, but with the potential of breaking under the stress of internal and external forces. What happens underneath the surface of the merger—cultural alignment, employee

---

[14] Information from an image source: HP & Cendix.com: Navigating Icebergs

communications, and skirmishes between leaders with clashing egos—is so important that it could have scuttled the entire process. HP, though, knew this, and they made sure not to let these key issues sink the integration process. The results speak for themselves, as HP's revenue drastically increased after the merger. This merger was a significant reason for 62% growth in revenue in two years, and it continued to have sustained growth for several years. Strategic analysis in identifying as an acquisition target, careful planning, successful cultural integration, and an open communication plan all combined to help HP become the leading technology company in the world at that time.

Even companies that have successfully merged, though, aren't guaranteed to succeed every time. Consider HP's next merger.

Not long after the HP-Compaq merger, HP merged with Electronic Data Systems (EDS) for $13.9 billion in 2008. EDS was not widely considered to be on the same trajectory as Compaq. Four years later, in 2012, because of internal decisions combined with the global economic climate, HP confirmed it was writing off about $8 billion after the drop in EDS's value. From my understanding, this means that EDS's market value was $8 billion less than it was when HP bought EDS. In other words, after the merger, 60 percent of the company's financial value was wiped away. Instead of making money for HP, it ended up costing them significantly.

As you can see, HP-Compaq merger contributed to 62% growth in two years, in contrast, HP-EDS merger caused 60% loss of financial value post-merger. Why did the EDS merger fail while the Compaq merger succeeded? In my interview with Craig Edland, Global Product Manager of Security & Privacy at EDS, he shared an enlightening perspective about the integration process. He painted a picture of two companies with very different cultures. HP was a product company, and EDS was a service company; as a result, the two organizations had different mindsets and cultures. HP was transaction-focused, and EDS, being a service company, had a servant-leadership culture. Their cultures were too dissimilar to blend harmoniously, and these cultural mismatches undermined the companies' best-laid strategic plans.

This goes to show that even successful companies—and even those well-versed in the details of M&A integration—can fail when cultures are incompatible.

Emotional Stages in M&A Integration Process

In researching the importance of managing emotions during the M&A process, I had the opportunity to interview Carolyn Taylor, one of the world's foremost experts in corporate culture transformation and the CEO of *Walking the Talk*, an organization that helps businesses manage cultural change. Taylor has conducted workshops with over 50,000 leaders, facilitated 200 culture-change journeys, consulted on fifteen M&As, and coached sixty CEOs, over the past three decades. Taylor is one of the most respected experts on the emotional aspects of mergers. She told me, "I have found mergers to bring out very tribal instincts in almost everyone involved. People's view of their own tribe is enhanced, while the other is seen in a negative light." Taylor elaborated that at the time of the merger, a strong sense of loyalty arises. Employees feel like they have a unique culture and a distinct way of doing things; they behave, in short, like a family. Co-workers may not always get along, but when someone attacks them, they jump to the defense of their family members.

As the collaboration begins, this mindset starts to shift. Taylor described a client who glorified their company's process and people. During the merger, they wanted the other company to play by the "right" rules, which happened to be the ones they were most familiar with—as opposed to probing what each side does well and integrating the best practices of each. Taylor took care to note these are emotional and almost unconscious reactions, not necessarily logical ones. That's why the teams on both sides have to work hard to integrate as each side navigates this emotional journey.

Taylor describes five mental models that can potentially exist during a merger, and people have to go through at least the first four to reach the point where the culture becomes an asset:

Mindsets During an M&A

1	My way is the only way.	Ignorance that other organisations are not like mine.
2	My way is the best way.	Arrogance, superiority.
3	You have some good ways too.	Understanding, objective observation, respect.
4	Let me learn from your ways.	Open-ness, benefits realisation.
5	Let's build a new way together.	New identity, best of both.

Source (and Copyright): Walking the Talk, Carolyn Taylor

As Taylor pointed out to me, in an average integration process, six months is an ideal timeframe to transition from level 1 all the way to level 5. According to her, almost without exception, when companies are stuck at levels 1 and 2 for more than six months, the number one reason is emotional: arrogance, tribalism, and unwillingness to learn from the other party are getting in the way. **"If you wait until things have settled down, you will find that a de facto culture has emerged which may not produce the best outcome for the future performance of the business."** — Taylor said. Many companies let that happen instead of deliberately creating a new combined culture. When de facto culture and processes are formed like this, later you may find that you are forced to relinquish some of your decision-making power. Which may not be a problem for you, but it undermines companies core values.

For that reason, it isn't enough for business leaders to "let things play out" and assume results will follow. It takes genuine leadership to manage the emotions of employees and communicate throughout this process to ensure a successful transition through stages 1 through 5. Taylor agrees, adding, "The people stream of a good integration team will address most of these emotions through change management planning." In other words, leaders of merging companies need to make concrete plans to help their employees transition from stubbornness to acceptance, and even excitement, for the company's plans.

What are the elements of a good change management plan? "Involvement; frequent, factual communication; and speed are the basis of good change management during mergers," Taylor says. "These all serve to reduce uncertainty and the emotions associated with being in the dark." Managers need to expect employees to have negative emotions during mergers. Insecurity, anger, grief, and even arrogance are the most common negative emotions leaders will encounter during integration. Rather than dismissing employees' legitimate concerns and emotional reactions—no matter how negative they are—leaders have to account for these reactions and help employees process them so they can come out on the other side fully on-board with change.

Beyond clearly communicating about specific changes that will happen post-merger, you can also combat negative emotional reactions by inspiring your team. "Work on the vision and future will help to lift people out of their negative emotions and increase their excitement," says Taylor. Time is of the essence, so it's important to create a change management plan early in the integration process. As Taylor attests, "Most of the key decisions made in the first few months of integration have a cultural impact." Deciding which company's CEO will helm the new, combined company is as important as figuring out which aspects of each company's culture should be embraced or discarded. So, the earlier culture gets onto the agenda in a meaningful way, the better chance you have of ending up with a culture that will support future plans and deliver the benefits laid out in the original merger proposition.

Emotional States During an M&A

Insecure	Angry	Unvalued	Grieving	Arrogant
• Will I have a job? • Will I have to move? • Will I lose my friends, status, perks, and opportunities? • What will happen to my projects, plans, performance, and customers?	• Why did they do this? • Why is no-one consulting us? • How come those people are being more advantaged than me? • They're making a real mess of this.	• Doesn't anyone care about my customers, projects, plans, experience? • Why is no-one telling me anything? • How come I'm not in the "inner circle"?	• I don't want to lose our name, identity, team, rituals, friends.	• I'm better than them, we've come out on top here, we're invincible.

Source (and Copyright): Walking the Talk, Carolyn Taylor

So, what are the common elements of successful mergers when it comes to workplace culture? According to Taylor, good mergers are characterized by respect, valuing others' opinions, and curiosity.

Leaders, in other words, must respect the emotional responses of the entire team. Not everyone is going to be immediately excited by change—in fact, you can expect many to feel threatened by it. Know that going in and treat these emotional responses as legitimate; never minimize them or think less of employees for being anxious about a merger. Next, listen and value the opinions of the whole team. They might have excellent ideas about which aspects of the work culture should stay and which should go during the integration. Finally, be curious and prepare to learn. When integration starts, everyone has to keep an open mind as two cultures merge. **In differences, look for opportunities. Embedded differences in diversity trigger our emotions and push us to grow.** Explore how you can diversify your workplace with the new partnership.

How will you know if you've succeeded in managing emotions during an M&A.? If the business integration is successful, you'll be able to see it in the workplace and hear it from your employees, from the top to the bottom of the organization chart. Robert B. Reich, a former Secretary of Labor who served in the administrations of three presidents, calls it the "pronoun test." He said he asks front-line workers a few general questions about the company. If employees still use the word "they" or "them" to refer to their pre-merger companies, it clearly reveals disintegration and alienization. Using the "we" pronoun, in Reich's words, indicates that employees feel responsible for the company's future.

In other words, if you hear terms like "they" or "them," you're dealing with one kind of company. If you hear "we" or "us," you've got a different kind of company—a more successful one. *That's* how you'll know you successfully managed your employees' emotions during a merger or acquisition.

ONE Brand — Positioned for Customers and Investors

After the M&A integration, as the combined culture matures, so does the integrated brand in the eyes of stakeholders, customers and investors. If there is lack of synergy between groups and they still operate disjointedly, it doesn't stay as an internal matter these days. Customers and investors can sense it easily. Customers start to lose their confidence, and it lessens your company's value in the eyes of investors.

Hearing of integration, customers usually ask: What will be an impact on the ongoing projects? How will you protect my service? What will be different? Your customers expect a zero-disruption experience during and after the integration. If you want to protect your largest and important customer who contributes to your revenue and drives future growth, look inside your groups working on their projects. Are they still operating disjointedly?

If your company wants to attract investors, the company's market value can be significantly increased if your company is able to show a new combined culture and executive team alignment. It will improve your company's posture in the eyes of the investors. On the other hand, if the integration doesn't happen collaboratively in a timely manner, the valuation of your company can be downgraded.

The merger and acquisitions process, as we have seen, can be difficult, and not every business navigates it successfully. This should come as no surprise, given the intense emotions that accompany this process. Fortunately, the common pitfalls associated with M&As — negotiation errors, fear and greed, cultural mismatches, and poor communication are avoidable. Emotional stability in the combined entity is very important for a successful integration and operation. Managing the emotions of all stakeholders, from existing employees to new ones, from previous management to the new leadership team, is paramount during this process.

When companies merge or get acquired, certain changes are inevitable. The fact that differences exist between the cultures of the two organizations doesn't necessarily mean that failure is inevitable. Far from it—if the cultural integration and communication are strategically planned during the merger or acquisition, positive results will ensue. Using the power of emotional intelligence, you can ensure that everyone feels seen, valued, and cared for. Once you've managed your team's emotions and helped them understand why this M&A will bring a positive change, not a negative one, you'll have their buy-in, and you'll be on your way to a smooth, productive process.

However, no matter how well we plan our change or integration process, some changes can be too adverse in nature —so notably unexpected and sudden that it can shake us from the core. In the next chapter, we will explore how deliberate leaders can respond to some of the most adverse changes with resilience

Chapter 9

Building Adaptive Resilience

"The Best Response to Disaster is Resilience."

— Madeleine Albright

I still remember what time it was. It was 7:45 pm on a Wednesday in the spring of 2018. I had just come home from work, and I was in a great mood. I spent a few minutes relaxing. Then I was catching up and playing with my kids. My phone rang.

I answered, and I heard my sister screaming, "Brother, something has happened to our dad!"

"What happened?" I asked.

"I don't know, I got a call from his neighbor... dad has fainted or something. They're saying he is not responding."

I felt worried and helpless. My father lived far away with my partially disabled mom, with severe mobility limitations.

My sister said, "I will call his home phone again and see if someone picks up."

"Ok, do that," I replied. "In the meantime, I will start calling other neighbors to find out what they know," and I hung up in a hurry.

I called one of my parents' neighbors, and they said, "Your dad should be fine. We just saw him last night and had a great conversation with him. But I will check on him and call you back shortly."

That gave me some relief, but I remained concerned. I knew something wasn't right. While I was anxiously awaiting a call from the neighbor, my sister called again. She wasn't saying anything, only wailing. She couldn't answer any of my questions. She just kept crying, "Brother, brother…" and, after a long cry, she screeched, "our father is no more!" When she calmed down enough to speak, I learned that my dad had succumbed to a massive heart attack while he was asleep.

I remember standing in the middle of my family room as her words pierced my heart. Then I heard my little daughter behind me asking, "Dad, dad… what's wrong? Is everything OK...?"

When I received this shattering news about my father's death, I felt nothing at first, just numb and empty. Then, after several moments passed, I felt as if I was being cut in two. For what felt like hours, I was at a loss for words. I couldn't imagine my father was gone like this. Only four days ago, I had wished my mom and dad a happy wedding anniversary. My father had said he was looking forward to celebrating their golden anniversary in a few years.

My father was in excellent health and lived a very active life. He was a mathematician, a lifetime problem-solver, and, above all else, he was a loving, caring, and humble person. His originality always surprised everyone. He touched so many lives, and he inspired everyone around him. I knew he wasn't young, but the force of grief I felt after suddenly losing him was beyond all rationality.

The Last Page from my Dad's Notebook

$$= r\left\{\frac{d\theta}{ds} + \frac{dr}{ds}\cdot\frac{d\psi}{dr}\right\} = r\frac{d}{ds}(\theta+\psi) = r\frac{d\psi}{ds}$$

$$= \frac{r}{\rho} \quad \text{or} \quad \rho = r\frac{dr}{d\rho} \quad \underline{\text{Proved}}$$

$$p = r\sin\psi \;\Rightarrow\; \frac{dp}{dr} = 1\cdot\sin\psi + r\cos\psi\,\frac{d\psi}{ds}\cdot\frac{ds}{dr}$$

$$= r\frac{d\theta}{ds} + r\cdot\left(\frac{dr}{ds}\cdot\frac{ds}{dr}\right)\frac{d\psi}{ds} = r\frac{d}{ds}(\theta+\psi) = r\frac{d\psi}{ds}$$

$$p = r\sin\psi \;\Rightarrow\; \frac{dp}{dr} = \sin\psi + r\frac{d\cos\psi}{dr} = r\frac{d\theta}{ds} + r\cos\psi\frac{d\psi}{dr}$$

$$= r\frac{d}{ds}\left\{\theta + \frac{dr}{ds}\cdot\frac{d\psi}{dr}\right\} = r\frac{d\psi}{ds} = \frac{r}{\rho}$$

$$p = r\sin\psi \;\Rightarrow\; \frac{dp}{dr} = 1\cdot\sin\psi + r\cos\psi\,\frac{d\psi}{ds}\cdot\frac{ds}{dr}$$

$$= r\frac{d\theta}{ds} + r\cdot\left(\frac{dr}{ds}\cdot\frac{ds}{dr}\right)\frac{d\psi}{ds} = r\frac{d}{ds}(\psi+\theta) = \frac{r\,d\psi}{ds}$$

$$= r/\rho$$

Q Prove $\quad \rho = p + \dfrac{d^2p}{d\psi^2}$

Q Prove that the pedal equation of $\dfrac{x^2}{a^2} + \dfrac{y^2}{b^2} - 1 = 0 \quad \text{①}$

$$\text{is} \quad \frac{1}{p^2} = \frac{1}{a^2} + \frac{1}{b^2} - \frac{r^2}{a^2 b^2}$$

$$x^2 + y^2 - r^2 = 0$$

$$\phi\;\frac{x^2}{a^2} + \frac{y^2}{b^2} - \frac{1}{p^2}$$

He was still working on mathematical problems, which he really enjoyed, a few hours before he died. This shows how active and alert he still was. Scary thought, isn't it? How life can be so fragile.

In the months after my father's death, I had a completely irrational fear of falling asleep and never waking. I also had an immense sense of guilt, a haunting feeling it was my fault for not spending more time with him before he passed. I felt horrible that I hadn't been able to say goodbye. But, for the most part, I didn't even have time to mourn him because I realized how much our lives were about to change due to his sudden death, and I needed to prepare myself for all that was to come. I am the elder of my two siblings. I knew I had to shift my focus to the current challenges I had to face. I had a new and immediate responsibility: to take care of our disabled mother, who had been bedridden for seven years. Her well-being and care became our primary focus. We brought my mom to our home right after my dad passed away and hired an experienced caregiver for her. I interviewed about a dozen caregivers, and Frankie turned out to be one of the best hires I have made. When I was interviewing her, she told me that, with the right care and therapy, one day my mom would walk again. Knowing my mom was bedridden for several years, I was skeptical about that.

Through diligent care at home, the miracle happened. It took weeks to recover from the atrophy caused by her immobility, but she did recover. She started to regain control. Her brain started to give the signal that her body began to obey again. In three months, my mom was walking with the support of a walker. Today my mother is not only walking but has recovered beyond anyone's expectations.

After we sorted through the immediate challenges, I turned to my own emotional healing. I started to connect with people who had lost a loved one and had gone through a similar journey. Understanding how others developed their resilience helped me a lot. When I was sharing memories with others, I started to see a future where I could be happy again.

Despite the emotional progress I was making, negative thoughts nagged at me in the years following his death. Even as I felt myself healing in some ways, I was also heading down a rabbit hole of negative self-talk. *Maybe I should have done something. Maybe I should have said something. Maybe it's my fault.* Contemplating what-ifs became mind-numbing. Not only I was thinking about the loss of my father, but also everything that stemmed from that loss: when my father died, my mother lost her best friend of 47 years; his siblings, too, lost a guardian, mentor, and friend.

Slowly, I started to challenge my negative thought patterns. It's not easy, and I am still grieving. I still miss my dad. I miss him every single day. But, as I have found, pain is a wonderful teacher. This life-changing incident made me see everything in a new light and made me more emotionally resilient. I realized it's a fact of life—I am not alone, everyone loses parents. But when I met people who had lost their young child, spouses, or significant others, I could imagine the force of grief *they* may have. My personal incident made me a more empathetic person. Another lesson I learned on my path to healing was that every emotion is fleeting. Even the strongest, most overwhelming emotions lose their power with time. Our bodies and minds have a natural ability to heal. If we give ourselves enough time to process our emotions, we can come out on the other side stronger, no longer at the mercy of negative thoughts and feelings.

After I had more time to reflect on my healing journey, I started to think about how these coping mechanisms could be applied to other challenges, whether in our personal lives or in the business world. Many events we need to overcome in life and in business can cause turbulence. As I researched adaptive-resilience models to better understand my own healing process, I revisited the Kubler-Ross Change Curve, which describes the stages of emotions experienced by a person approaching death or surviving a loved one's death. In this model, as you may know, the five stages are — denial, anger, bargaining, depression, and acceptance. It's a generic change-management model and can be applied to adverse business situations as well. This model can be effectively used by business leaders to help their workforce build adaptive resilience and navigate difficult workplace changes.

I want to encourage you to take a moment to consider how the phases of the Kubler-Ross model might apply to a situation you have found yourself in. Can you recall a time when challenging circumstances led you from shock to denial to frustration? Have you ever felt healing happen, when you moved from depression to experimenting to a decision to embrace change? Have you ever experienced the feeling of integration, in which you adapted to changes and moved forward with a renewed sense of purpose?

Let's consider the M&A integration process we reviewed in the previous chapter. As we saw, when companies merge or get acquired, certain changes are inevitable and can be disruptive. To understand how employees react to the M&A process, we can look to the world of psychiatry. This general rubric can be applied to the emotional journey of employees during the M&A emotional journey as well.

Let's consider a hypothetical acquisition of Metrolite Inc by Globex Corporation LLC[15]. John and Sally, longtime Metrolite employees, learn about their company's acquisition, and they first react with **shock.** "I thought we were a stable and self-sustainable company with solid funding," says Sally. "So did I," replies John. "Does this mean we'll lose our jobs or have to work under a different management?" Shock quickly turns into **denial**, with Sally saying, "This has to be a rumor. I don't believe the deal is going to go through."

When it becomes clear that the acquisition is indeed moving forward, John becomes **frustrated**. "Everything was working fine before Globex came along! Why do we need to learn all these new processes?" he complains. These only feeds Sally's **depression**, and she says, "This is so sad. We have such a great team here, and Globex is undermining all our efforts."

Fortunately for both companies, the leaders of Metrolite Inc and Globex Corporation had a comprehensive integration plan that accounted for the emotional responses of their employees. Soon, John

---

[15] These two are hypothetical business names.

and Sally are open to **experimenting** with the new culture. "Let's give this a try," Sally tells John, and John agrees: "OK, let's see if the new way of doing things works." After a few weeks of embracing flexibility, John reaches a positive **decision**: "I can make this work. Let's commit to the new way of doing things." And just like that, **integration** is successful, as Sally tells John, "I'm feeling so much better now. We can do this!"

Kubler-Ross Change Curve

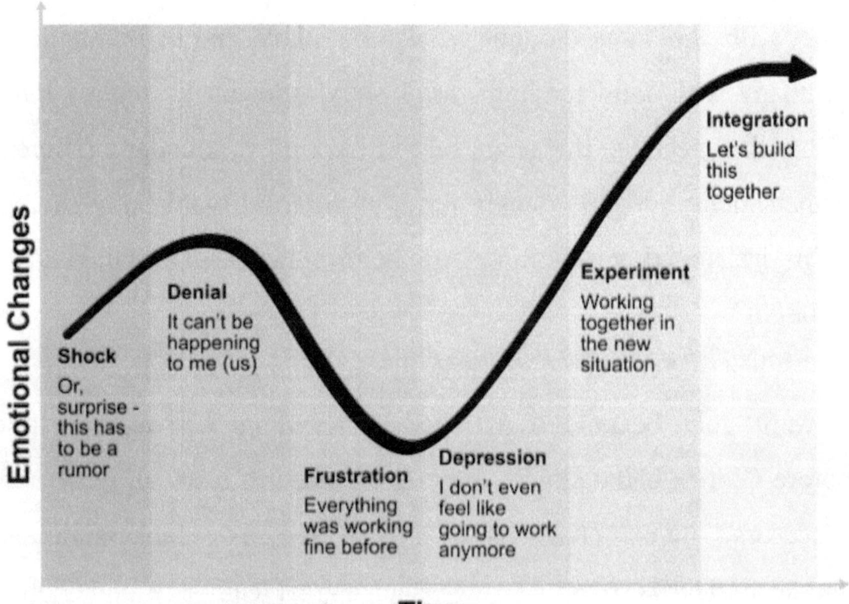

Resilient Leadership

My point is that such model and process of acceptance and integration is flexible and universal: it applies to so many of our experiences, and, chances are, you have lived through the phases the model outlines. Since the great depression in 1929, every few years, we face a financial crisis. In early 2000 recession, there were sharp decline in most businesses. It is considered the most significant downturn since the Great Depression. As the economy and many businesses were still recovering from that recession, in 2008, the collapse of the housing market fueled by easy credit, low-interest rates, insufficient regulation, and toxic subprime mortgages — led to the economic crisis again. As I write this book, we are going through one of the worst global pandemics in human history and still recovering as a society. The reality of life post-COVID-19 has not fully sunk in yet, and its consequences for our community, economy, businesses, and organizations will play out over the years. What we do know with certainty is that the pandemic has left immeasurable suffering in its wake. What we have learned from these economic downturns and business adversities, resilient leaders have the ability to sustain their energy level under pressure, cope with disruptive changes and adapt.

Recognizing the Emotional Lives of Your Team

I wanted to learn more about how we can recover from the challenges life throws at us, and in my research, I had the opportunity to interview George Lindenfeld, Ph.D., a clinical psychologist, and author whom I have known through a common friend. Dr. Lindenfeld is a founder of the Medical Psychology Center in Asheville, North Carolina, which specializes in evaluating and treating traumatic life experiences. He has done extensive work in the area of post-traumatic stress disorder (PTSD). What Dr. Lindenfeld described applies directly to the business world, and I want to share it with you.

In our society, when people experience acute depression, they often resort to medication to treat the symptoms. But, as Dr. Lindenfeld reminded me, "the medication doesn't alter the brain circuitry." The beneficial effects of the medication are temporary. As part of his practice working with veterans, he has monitored ongoing memory research and pursued the non-invasive potential of neuro-acoustical intervention, which led him to develop a treatment process called RESET Therapy (Reconsolidation Enhancement through Stimulation of Emotional Triggers). This therapy has demonstrated rapid and enduring remission of the emotional aspects of PTSD or any other trauma. He shared research on Quantitative EEG (qEEG), an analysis of digitized EEG. In lay terms, this sometimes is also called "Brain Mapping." The results, he found, were far and away more long-lasting than any medication used to treat PTSD and any depression. Dr. Lindenfeld actually saw people's damaged neural circuitry partially begin to reverse.

This has profound applications in business world. Dealing with any trauma—whether it's the loss of a loved one or being passed up for a promotion—requires adaptive resilience. It should come as no surprise that trauma applies to the workplace just as it does to our personal lives. **After all, we spend so much of our adult lives at work, and part of being an effective leader is recognizing the emotional lives of your team.** Trauma is contagious, and it can spread within an organization among colleagues in close proximity. This is why it is so important to build adaptive resilience culture at the organizational level.

Business Leaders at Heightened Risk of Emotional Turmoil

Emotional trauma is probably much more widespread in the workplace than many imagine. Consider the work of Dr. Daniel Amen, a psychiatrist, and brain-disorder specialist, who and his crew studied 175,000 brain scans. He said[16], "Some of the most highly motivated individuals that we have scanned, such as CEOs of companies, have had significantly increased activities in their basal ganglia," which refers to a group of subcortical nuclei in our brains responsible for executive functions, behaviors, and emotions. Dr. Amen and Lisa Routh wrote in a book they co-authored[17]: One of our theories is that excessive basal ganglia activity maybe associated with heightened anxiety or with increased motivation. If you do not use increased basal ganglia activity to get things done, you are more likely to feel anxiety and tension. Some people can harness this increased energy and channel it productively to become the movers in our society. But they may also suffer from intense inner turmoil.

Dr. Amen's research suggests, in other words, that business leaders might be at heightened risk of experiencing emotional turmoil.

---

[16] In Dr. Daniel Amen's bestseller book - **Change Your Brain, Change Your Life**
[17] Book: Healing Anxiety and Depression

I believe it is imperative that business leaders build adaptive resilience to the challenges they are likely to face throughout their careers.

I am not writing about these theories to recommend business leaders seek therapy. The point I am trying to make is this: *you can train your brain.* Several new studies have shown that the brain works like a muscle. [18]Our brain gets stronger and changes when we use it. Scientists have been able to prove how our brain grows and gets stronger when we learn. We know when we lift weights, our muscles get stronger and grows. Likewise, our ability to be resilient in one area of life or business makes us stronger and makes emotionally resilient in other areas. This is adaptive resilience.

Use Stress Responses as a Resilience Mechanism

No one wakes up in the morning thinking, "I hope terrible things happen to me." But we have negative experiences all the time, and some traumatic incidents overwhelm the coping ability of an individual or group. These happen to us through no fault of our own. When negative experiences happen, chemicals are released in our body. This can make you twitch and sweat, and your mind will start racing. You become nervous and more tense.

Instead of viewing these bodily changes as a dreadful thing, what if you thought of these stress responses as your body preparing you to face a challenge? If you are breathing faster, it is okay–your heart is sending more oxygen to your brain. Keep breathing and let your mind

---

[18] According to an article published in Central Michigan University website (cmich.edu).

prepare to face the challenge and to make your stress response healthier. Next time you experience this stress response in your body, start breathing from your belly.

Furthermore, stress makes you more social and resilient. When stressed, our body releases a neuro-hormone called oxytocin. It's the same hormone released when you hug someone; that's why it's also called the "cuddle hormone." Oxytocin makes you do things that strengthen social bonds. It enhances your empathy, and it makes you want to contact your friends and family. It makes you want to support your loved ones and even your community. If your body is releasing oxytocin as a stress response, your mind motivates you to seek support and support your loved ones. That's why you will notice that people become more social during a national or world disaster. And, for the same reason, employees tend to become "tribal" during company's M&A process. Now, you can see the "science" behind the tribalism I mentioned in the previous chapter, "*Managing Emotions in Mergers & Acquisitions*". It's a positive thing, and when these emotions are channeled and managed well, the impact is profound.

Oxytocin functions not only in the brain. It also operates in your body. It protects your cardiovascular system from the effects of stress. It's also a natural anti-inflammatory; it helps your blood vessels stay relaxed during stressful conditions. The heart has a receptor for oxytocin, and these hormones help regenerate and heal from any stress-induced damage. So, this stress hormone oxytocin has the potential to strengthen your heart. All the benefits of this hormone are enhanced by social contact and social support. Social psychologist Shelley E. Taylor, Ph.D., who directs the UCLA Social Neuroscience Lab, labels this the "tend and befriend" response instead of the "fight or flight" response.

The bottom line is this: if you are under stress, and if you reach out to people either to seek support or to help others, you will recover faster from the stressful event, and you will be more stress resilient.

Adaptive Resilience Leadership

As I have said, adaptive resilience is one of the keys to successful leadership in any business venture. The ability to respond to challenges—and the ability to become stronger by facing challenges—is necessary for whatever line of work a leader finds themselves. Based on my research, I have distilled the most important lessons about adaptive resilience into four pieces of advice:

Avoid overreacting.

The ability to avoid over-reaction is an essential life skill that applies to the business world. According to author, educator, and radio preacher Charles Swindoll, "Life is 10% what happens to you and 90% how you react to it." Therefore, this ability lies within us, and we are in charge of our attitudes. It's not an easy attitude to change if you feel like it doesn't come naturally to you—but remember, the brain is a muscle, and by putting this habit into action, you can develop this skill.

When bad things happen, don't let the current situation

undermine your past positive experiences. Try to access your memory and apply those positive emotions to the current situation to try to take control of your response to the situation. The people you're interacting with, be they colleagues, employees, or customers, may be having a bad day, or there must be another side of the story you don't know about. When you encounter the negative emotions of others, always remember that you are the only person who controls your own emotions.

In times of crisis, remain authentic, and don't change your style. Don't forget why people have come to trust and follow you in the first place. Avoid any overreaction and keep your natural persona to create calm and focus. In adverse times, people crave familiarity.

Frame situations as challenges rather than problems.

Business requires constant creative problem-solving. Challenges never end. As soon as you solve one problem, another one emerges. Consider this common situation: you badly need to win that new contract, the one that will turn your business around or take your company to the next level of profitability. After a tedious and lengthy pre-sales process, you are awarded the contract. But it's not the straightforward win you thought it was—it turns out this client is difficult to work with.

So, it goes in the business world. Not all projects are enjoyable. Some customers often have unique needs. Many projects are difficult and demanding. Maybe you need to hire a new employee to do the job. Now you need to manage them and provide them with the right tools. But then, maybe your new employee creates new headaches you have to deal with. The problems keep multiplying, and each problem needs to be confronted. However, we often need to get away from thinking about everything as a problem and think about them as challenges. Problems can seem intractable, but challenges can be solved!

How can you deal with a multiplying series of challenges? When a problem is presented, asking "why" three times can get to the core of the matter. As I described in the previous chapter, I often ask three "why's" either to the party I am dealing with or to myself to get to the bottom of the real problem. Consider this example: a team member tells her manager, "I just can't close this sale." The manager, in turn, asks, "Why not?" The employee replies, "I'm just not connecting with the prospective client." The manager then asks, "Why aren't you connecting with them?" The employee responds, "I just don't have enough time to devote to fostering a relationship with them." The manager asks the third "why": "Why don't you have time to devote to the client?" The employee responds, "Because I'm overwhelmed preparing for the upcoming presentation."

What is happening here is that the manager is moving from a problem to a challenge. Problems can seem insurmountable—but challenges are solvable! Asking three "why's", in my experience, is an excellent way to build critical thinking skills.

Another way to think about reframing problems as challenges is the "Rose, Thorn, and Bud" approach. This is an excellent way to tag individual data points as roses (positives), thorns (negatives), and buds (opportunities). When your team or any other stakeholder is singling out a problem, you as a leader should show them the complete picture and remind them about the areas of opportunity or ideas yet to be explored. Not every challenge is a thorn—many are just buds or even roses, but we just don't realize it.

This shift in perspective requires attention, a conscious effort, and out-of-the-box thinking, but seeing the situation in a new light can pay dividends. As Albert Einstein said, "No problem can be solved from the same level of consciousness that created it." Innovation happens when we step back from the problem and view it from a different perspective.

Practice self-soothing techniques and develop the ability to relax deeply.

All things being equal, when you are able to self-soothe, you are more resilient and more powerful than those who haven't developed that skill yet. Everyone can benefit from self-soothing, deep breathing, and deep relaxation techniques. If you are a leader, the impact it will have on your organization is exponentially greater.

The following can help reduce the stress at the workplace or in life in general:

- Taking time to explore the meaning, purpose, and direction of your life and career.
- Volunteering or doing service work to help others and feel better about your own effectiveness and purpose. It can be a great way to connect with your community and network with

peer-leaders without any pressure of agenda.

- Enhancing connections in order to combat isolation.

Develop an ability to return to a baseline after a stressful event.

This gets to the core of building adaptive resilience at the physical and emotional levels. We not only need to find our individual emotional baselines we can return to after a stressful experience, but we also need to build communal, organizational resilience that allows every member of the team to recover.

When I'm feeling overwhelmed with anxiety or stress, one of the techniques I often use is power posture. This can be standing akimbo or standing in any posture that one mentally associates with being powerful. The idea is that the physical pose translates to feelings of confidence. Research has shown that standing in power posture for 20 minutes can increase confidence levels by 20 percent.

What Leaders Gain by Being Vulnerable

This may sound counterintuitive, but being vulnerable is a *strength*, not a weakness. Professor, researcher, and author Brené Brown argues that vulnerability is a sign of courage. It takes courage to be in touch with one's difficult and uncomfortable feelings—and to risk the feelings being exposed with uncertainty how they will be received. It is only by being vulnerable that we can grow as people— and help the people in our businesses and organizations grow.

I would argue that vulnerability is a requirement for all successful leaders. Those leaders who show their own emotions are the ones that can create an organizational environment that empowers employees, managers, and stakeholders to be open about their emotional difficulties. Through this process, problems can transform into surmountable challenges. The ability to ask others for help, admit mistakes, and share fears are assets, not weaknesses.

Through vulnerability comes adaptive resilience. It is only after a leader takes an honest look at their strengths, weaknesses, fears, and anxieties they can become stronger and more resilient.

We all go through periods of emotional difficulty. Whether it's losing a family member (as I did), a life-changing personal event, or dealing with organizational changes in a workplace - these situations don't happen in an emotional vacuum. Leaders who acknowledge their own emotions and the emotions of their employees are leaders who can build strong, adaptive organizations.

Ultimately, this is the most important aspect of resilience: it's not about an individual building their resilience, it's about the *organization as a whole* building adaptive resilience. A resilient organization is constantly reassessing its strengths and weaknesses and striving to improve. This all starts with leaders who are emotionally strong but still allow themselves to be vulnerable as the situation demands — which, in turn, allows the entire organization to be resilient.

Also, when it feels like your world is falling apart, care for yourself. Our brain has amazing plasticity for adaptability and renewal—we have to give it the chance to spring back. In the next chapter, we will discuss how we can apply mind-body intelligence in leadership — a new perspective on resilience for today's business leaders. Over the last 20 years, advances in neuroscience have revealed more surprising scientific evidence and data than ever before about how mind-body intelligence can be applied in leadership and the business world. If you have come with me this far, let's explore the last and final chapter, "Mind-Body Leadership" — which will empower you with simple and easy to follow tools and techniques to become more deliberate and intuitive leader.

Chapter 10

Leading with Mind-Body Intelligence

"You only get one mind and one body. And it's got to last a lifetime."

— Warren Buffett

In Warren Buffett's biography, *The Snowball*, author Alice Schroeder recounts a story Buffett shared with a group he was speaking to. As Buffett told it, a genie appeared to him at age 16 and offered him the car of his choice. But there's a catch, says the genie: His dream car would have to last a lifetime because it would be the last car Buffett would ever own. To understand how to care for the car, Buffett said he would be sure to read the manual "about five times," always keep his car garaged, and fix even the smallest dents or scratches right away to protect it from rusting. "I would baby that car because it would have to last a lifetime," Buffett tells the group.

Then Buffett drives home a lesson that pertains to the business of life and the two things we should never neglect: "You only get one mind and one body. And it's got to last a lifetime. Now, it's very easy to let them ride for many years. But if you don't take care of that mind and that body, they'll be a wreck 40 years later, just like the car would be. It's what you do right now, today, that determines how your mind and body will operate 10, 20, and 30 years from now."

Often, we use the word "mind" and "brain" interchangeably. But let's dig deeper. A brain is a physical, tangible organ responsible for a host of physiological and cognitive processes, but then what is mind? When we talk about the mind, we're talking about the thoughts, feelings, and emotions we experience. The brain is the physical organ most associated with the mind, but the mind is not confined to the brain, which I will explain later in this chapter. You can think of the mind as the software and the brain as its hardware. If you want to run sophisticated software, you must optimize the hardware. If you're going to stretch your mind and embrace the Growth Mindset[19] to become an effective leader, you have to improve and optimize your physical brain. Later in this chapter, I will guide you through scientifically proven ways to tap into the brain's hidden potential.

As we've seen, the brain influences the mind, but the body and mind are also deeply interconnected. The mind indeed controls the body, but when we use our body in a certain way, it also affects our mind. I want you to, right now, do a little audit of your body. Are you making yourself smaller, hunched over this book as you are reading this? Are you crossing your legs? Are you holding your arms? What we do with our bodies—how we hold ourselves—affects our testosterone and cortisol levels which in turn affect the state of our mind. For example, when we smile, this sends a signal to the brain to feel happy. When you take a brisk walk or run for a few minutes, you

---

[19] Famous psychologist and Stanford University professor Carol Dweck coined the term "Growth Mindset" to describe the belief that intelligence can be developed.

can feel the shift in your state of mind.

Over the last 20 years, advances in neuroscience have revealed more scientific evidence and data than ever before about how the mind and body affect each other. This evidence comes from brain science, bioengineering, cellular level tissue analysis, and biochemical analysis of hormones and neurotransmitters. There are many body-brain models and tools backed by scientific evidence available today. We will review some of the most effective models in the domain of leadership and management. This knowledge and insight is incredibly helpful for educating and training leaders. It's essential that as a leader, you understand and model how to treat your own body and mind to promote positive, measurable effects on performance at work.

The Human Brain and Emotions

As a computer scientist, I have had a front-row seat on the long and complex journey of the world of IT architecture as it evolved from mainframes to mobile over the years, and the rate of change shows no signs of slowing. It took computer scientists decades to build supercomputers that could match the human brain's capacity for information storing, processing, and retrieval; still, these supercomputers are not even close to matching the powers and abilities of a real human brain. Even with a million processors, the most powerful supercomputers can only approach 1 percent of the scale of the human brain, and that's with a lot of simplifying assumptions. So, what is it that makes the human brain so special and unique?

Our brain is constantly processing information. Experts estimate that between 60,000 to 80,000 thoughts pass through an adult's brain in a single day. This doesn't mean, however, that we're always having meaningful thoughts. According to research conducted by [20]Harvard psychologists Killingsworth and team, our minds wander on average 47% of the time—that's almost half of our lives we are missing. Most of these thought processes are automatic. It is only when you need to focus on something that you become aware of your thoughts and able to channel them. The brain is always working, even if we aren't controlling the flow of our thoughts. Consider what happens to the brain when we are asleep. While we are sleeping, our brains are doing much more than getting ready for the next day. Researchers at the University of Rochester found that our brains are busy cleaning out harmful waste materials that build up during our waking lives. That's not to mention the mental activity of dreaming, which we do, on average, two hours each night. So, your mind is continually working or wandering. You may wonder how it is possible for our brain to continuously process such a massive volume of information. To answer this question, we can't underestimate the power of the human brain. Among all animals, humans have the largest brains relative to our body size. Although your brain is just three pounds of soft, tofu-like tissue, it has about 1.1 trillion cells and contains about 86 billion nerve cells called neurons. These neurons simultaneously fire and transmit signals to thousands of destinations. Our brain is like a living

---

[20] Harvard psychologists Matthew Killingsworth and Daniel T. Gilbert

supercomputer capable of processing a multitude of information every second.

Although we need not go to the details of brain anatomy here, if we consider ourselves as thought leaders or deliberate leaders, we need to understand the neuroscience behind emotional intelligence. Emotions we have discussed throughout this book are controlled and managed by the part of the brain called the "prefrontal cortex" — like a control center and is also called the "emotional brain". This area is involved during emotion regulation and helps guide our actions.

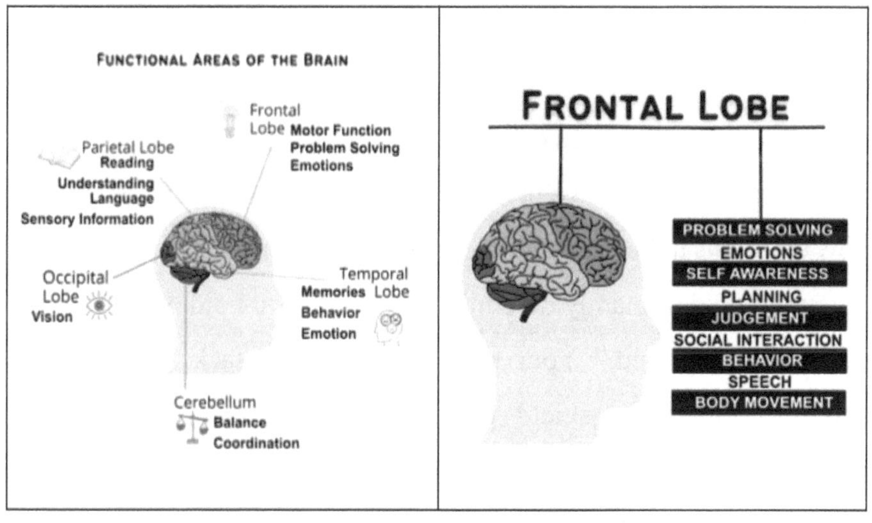

Are You a Left-Brain or Right-Brain Leader?

To understand how we can use the power of neuroplasticity to become better leaders, let's consider a basic breakdown you're likely familiar with: the left brain and the right brain. The human brain is separated into two cerebral hemispheres, left and right, which execute different functions. Because of this, left-handed people's brains function somewhat differently from their right-brained counterparts.

My daughter is naturally left-handed, and we didn't try to force her into using her right hand. We didn't realize she was a lefty until she went to kindergarten. At first, writing was difficult for her until a teacher put her pencil in her other hand, and she took off scribbling! Her right brain appears to be more dominant, where creativity and intuition are centered. She is more inclined to follow her creative flow.

It's very likely many writers, musicians, artists, and other creators tend to be left-handed. Emotions like happiness, pride, and anger come from the left side of the brain, and emotions associated with avoidance, like disgust and fear, come from the right brain. One historical theory put forward to explain the primacy of right-handedness is sometimes called the Sword and Shield Theory[21]. This theory states, the way we perform actions with our hands determines how emotions are organized in our brains. Depending on which hand you use, you dominantly determine what side you hold, your "sword" versus your "shield." Your sword is used to attack "an approach action," while your shield protects you, "an avoidance action." Therefore, approach emotions are housed in the dominant hemisphere, while avoidant ones are housed in the non-dominant one.

A brain scan study conducted by MIT researchers suggests that entrepreneurs tap both sides of their brains when making decisions. Dr. Mary Lou Décosterd, author of *Right Brain/Left Brain Leadership*, explains that the most influential leaders are those who can fluidly shift their leadership style in specific circumstances, where

---

[21] Proposed by the great 19th Century British writer Thomas Carlyle

one side of the brain might attain better results than the other. Such "hybrid" leaders who know when to shift between the two forms of thinking can make more sound decisions and have deeper level of intuition. Many books have described how playing board games, video games, and using apps can help you tap into both sides of your brain.

Additionally, here are three simple tips for developing and using both sides of your brain. You can incorporate these tips into your daily routine:

Practice using your non-dominant hand throughout the day.

When you use your phone or dining utensils, when you use a tool or do a chore, or when you use that TV remote, try using your non-dominant hand. This will, in turn, engage your non-dominant brain. This is the easiest way to engage your whole brain, and it requires no additional time to learn. There are positive side effects of this change, too: it may prevent carpal tunnel since you are not over-using the nerves in just one dominant hand. Also, using your non-dominant hand for doorknobs and bathrooms may even help minimize the spread of germs and viruses because you are unlikely to touch your face with that hand.

Change your physical environment to engage the other side of your brain.

If your work primarily involves left-brain activity (report writing, project tracking, research, etc.), decorate your physical space with art and listen to different types of music. Making these easy tweaks to your surroundings will allow you to engage your non-dominant brain.

Make thoughtful observations during your work.

Thinking up a strategy, visualizing it, and immediately implementing it is the right brain's delight. Let your right brain visualize the end result. Then, engage the left brain by identifying all the tactical steps necessary to complete a project. Doing this regularly will strengthen your powers of observation.

The Three Brains of Great Leaders

Have you ever heard someone say, "Don't lose your head over the situation," "My heart is broken," or "My gut instinct is..."? These phrases reflect the different ways we think and feel. Buried in these colloquial phrases are three ways of knowing and feeling: the head, the heart, and the gut.

These three knowledge paths are backed up by over 3,000 years of wisdom. Modern neuroscience has revealed that we have more complex and functional neural networks than exist in the "head brain" alone. The head functions well when things are clear, quantifiable, and tangible, but business is not always like that. The heart thrives on trusting relationships, following emotional connections, or being careful. Adaptive leadership requires new levels of self-awareness and self-regulation for integrating head-based cognitive intellect with heart-based values and gut-based instincts. Furthermore, guts allow digesting complex experiences before taking bold action in business.

Your Three Brains

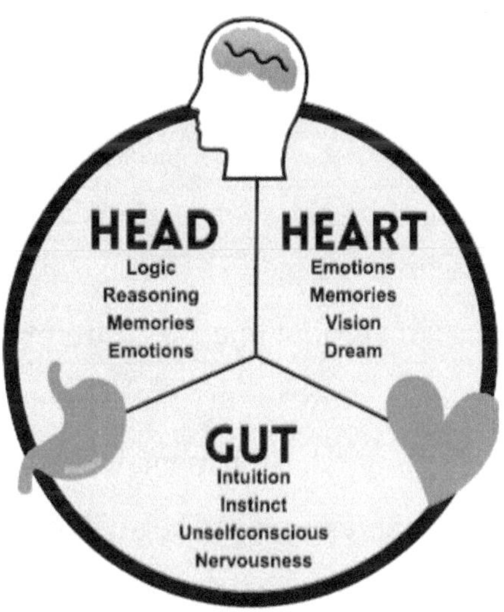

Many scientists believe microbiome is an intermediary between the food we take and our brains. For example, eating chocolate, as we all know, tends to make us feel good. Our microbiome is partially responsible for relaying that feeling to our brain. The good news is, unlike the genome, microbiomes can be modified by eating right, as we'll see later in this chapter.

Bringing together neuroscience, behavioral modeling, and cognitive linguistics, [22] Soosalu and team introduced a new and profound tool called mBraining (or mBIT, which stands for Multiple Brain Integration Techniques) for leaders and managers. It is a model of how we can use the complex, adaptive, and functioning neural networks of the brain, heart, and gut. The latest neuroscience has

---

[22] Grant Soosalu, and Marvin Oka. Soosalu is a trainer and writer with expertise in leadership, coaching, psychology, behavioral modeling, and applied physics. Marvin Oka has a specialization in leading-edge behavioral change technologies and research.

found that both the heart and the gut have the same kind of neurons as found in the brain. They even behave and function in the same way as neurons in the head brain by thinking and storing memories. The three brains communicate using the vagus nerve[23] that runs through your body.

Our guts, meanwhile, are made of over 100 trillion bacteria and about 100 million nerve cells that line the gastrointestinal tract. Recent scientific research has shown our gut bacteria produce many chemicals that affect our mood. Both mental and physical health, from Alzheimer's disease to depression, can be affected by the health of our guts. It's a myth that most of our serotonin (known as the happy chemical) is in our brain. The fact is, approximately 95 percent of our body's serotonin is actually found within the gut. GABA, another neurotransmitter that improves mood, is also often present in our gut. Serotonin and GABA are both released from "good bacteria" promoted by a healthy diet. On the other hand, "bad gut" bacteria have been linked to neuroimmune and neuroinflammatory diseases such as Alzheimer's, multiple sclerosis, and Parkinson's disease.

Neuroscience has revealed that sophisticated and functional neural networks constitute "brains" housed in our head, heart, and gut. According to Soosalu and team - this lends scientific credibility to the growing body of leadership literature showing how the world's best companies are guided by leaders who can tap into the intelligence of their head, heart, and guts. Combining these neuroscience findings

---

[23] Historically called the pneumogastric nerve.

with behavioral modeling research conducted by the authors, several key insights have been found about the roles of the heart and gut brains for adaptive and generative leadership.

Consciously Changing Your Brain Function

Have you ever had a strategic executive decision to make where the best options are not very obvious, the ethics aren't clear, and the consequences could affect other people? How do you determine which decision is the right one? And how do you develop a habit of making better decisions, time and time again? In most business decisions, you are likely to focus your attention on one of two methods: tactical or strategic. Tactical decisions favor expedient actions aimed at giving you what you want and giving others what they wish, rapidly and efficiently. On the other hand, strategic decisions require fundamental solutions with longer-term and broader benefits. These two patterns of mental activity are associated with two parts of the prefrontal cortex — dorsal (higher) for the strategic and ventral (lower) for the tactical.

You can choose where to focus your attention, and this choice will, over time, affect the physical makeup of your brain. Psychologist Donald Hebb discovered this principle, called Self-Directed Neuroplasticity, in the 1950s, and his findings have been popularly summarized as **"Neurons that fire together wire together,"** also called Hebb's Law. In other words, thinking patterns are likely to repeat the more you use them, and they may even become automatic. When Hebb published his theory, neuroscience didn't have those advanced tools, probes, and neuro-imaging techniques like CT scans and MRI. With the benefit of today's research tools, his argument has been vindicated. Think of it like this: the more you engage in a particular pattern of thought — for example, tactical thinking, the stronger its associated neural circuit becomes. Another saying is "practice makes perfect," which is another way of stating Hebb's Law. Next time you are dealing with a problematic vendor or customer service representative who puts you on hold for 15 minutes, try suppressing your anger and try to handle the situation tactfully. In doing so, you will be deepening the neural grooves, so to speak, that promote calmness and patience. Over time, due to Self-Directed Neuroplasticity, these ways of thinking and behaving will become automatic.

Mind, Body, and Leadership

Today's complex business environment requires a new type of leader. Being qualified and knowledgeable is not enough. Leaders must be adaptable, focused, and resilient to be effective amid the increasingly distracting and chaotic world of the twenty-first century business organization. The only way to achieve this is to balance your mind, body, and soul. Fortunately, we have the power to make our brains healthy. "Science has revealed the surprising truth that you can do more to make your brain healthier than any other part of your body," according to Dr. Sandra Chapman, chief director of the Center for BrainHealth at the University of Texas at Dallas.

As described earlier, over the last two decades, advances within healthcare and neuroscience have revealed more hard evidence than ever before about what's going on in our body and mind. The three elements of humans — mind, body, and soul — significantly contribute to leadership success. Here are a few key ways leaders can help themselves and their teams to stay healthy in body, mind, and soul.

Understand the basics of the body and mind.

Recall Warren Buffet's story that opened this chapter. Think of your body as the car that has to last a lifetime. You need to understand how it works, read the manual several times, and always keep the car garaged and fix even the smallest dents or scratches immediately to protect it from rusting. Your body and mind are continually changing. Neither your body nor your mind will be the same when you wake up tomorrow morning. The more you know about your body, the better you can take care of it. Unfortunately, our healthcare system is not designed to be people-centered; it is profit-centered and not focused on prevention. You have to be the "program manager" of your physical and mental health. Understand how your body and mind work and promote this awareness throughout your company.

To keep your brain sharp, active, and stimulated in the workplace, consider these tips:

- As a leader, never stop solving problems. Always keep a few tactical, problem-solving tasks for yourself, instead of delegating them.
- Spend time each day reading, writing new content, or both.

- Never stop learning. Go to a lecture, seminar, or try to acquire a new skill.
- Play memory games, board games (chess is one of the best), card games, or video games.
- Take on a new hobby that requires you to focus. I will talk more about this later in this book.

You are what you eat. [24]

This old adage has stood the test of time. According to Dr. Drew Ramsey, a medical doctor, psychiatrist, and author, our brain activity burns 20% of what we eat. Researchers have even discovered that certain foods promote certain types of thinking. For example, foods that boost brain health can attenuate neuroinflammation, reduce stress, and enhance neuroplasticity. Therefore, if we want to improve our cognitive function, we need to be conscious of what we're consuming. Consider adding more plant-based foods to your diet to improve your overall health. Eating a brain-boosting diet can support both short- and long-term brain function. Some of the best brain foods are berries, almonds, avocados, broccoli, kale, dark chocolate, turmeric, omega-3 fatty acids, fish or fish oil, olive oil, oysters, and eggs. The gut microbiome loves fiber and fermented food, and these are readily available, rich resources of antioxidants, curcumin, and vitamins that our brain needs. Recent research suggests these may prevent brain shrinkage and delay cognitive decline.

---

[24] In 1942, the nutritionist Victor Lindlahr, published *You Are What You Eat: How to Win and Keep Health with Diet.*

Sylvia Hatzer[25], an 82-year-old woman in UK, had dementia and couldn't even recognize her son. Sylvia had also phoned the police accusing her caregiver of kidnapping her. As bad as things got, she made specific changes to her diet that essentially paused her dementia. It had such a dramatic impact on Sylvia's condition that the Alzheimer's Society began sharing her recipes. You may be curious to know what was added to her diet. Sylvia began incorporating blueberries, walnuts, broccoli, kale, spinach, sunflower seeds, green tea, oats, sweet potatoes, and dark chocolate with a high percentage of cacao. These are not new brain diets, but it's one so many of us neglect to follow.

The brain food I mentioned above is based on the general recommendation by doctors, scientists, and nutritionists. This is not a book about diet and nutrition, of course, but I must warn you these so-called "brain foods" may not work for everyone. You need to be aware of foods you are allergic to and how your body reacts to them. When I interviewed self-made billionaire Naveen Jain, from his personal experience and eating habits, he cautioned me about what I think is the right food for me. His company, Viome, is an artificial-learning engine designed to analyze gut data and aggregate all the biological data collected. After I interviewed him, I was so eager to learn about my own microbiome profile. I ordered my lab test with Viome. When my result came back, I just stood up, stunned by a revelation. It said that my *"microbiome contains tropical soda apple mosaic virus,*

---

[25] According to *The Mirror* (UK based news website — mirror.co.uk).

which is known to infect apples. Since plant viruses in microbiome have been associated with an inflammatory response, it is recommended for you to avoid apples." Like many people, I used to believe in the proverb "an apple a day keeps the doctor away." All my life I have eaten apples and I love them. But, based on Viome's recommendation, I stopped eating apples. Since I started following microbiome dietary recommendation, I feel significant positive changes in my body and moods.

From my Microbiome's test result by Viome:

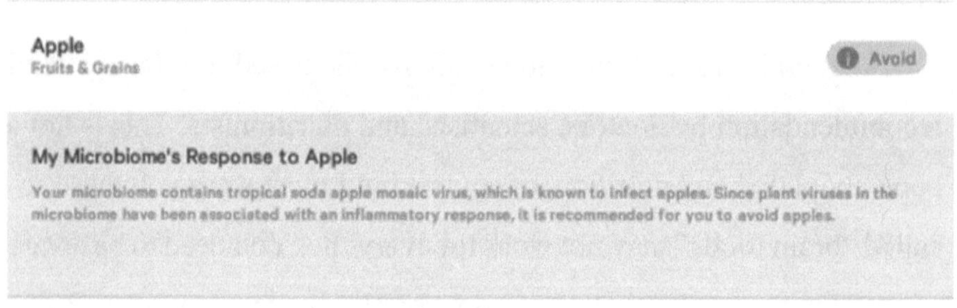

While I am not recommending you should get your Microbiome test done, you need to know what food works for you and what doesn't.

Sound sleep can make you a sound leader.

In an interview, Amazon founder Jeff Bezos discussed the importance of sleep. "I get eight hours of sleep. I think better, I have more energy, my mood is better," he said. "As a senior executive, you get paid to make a small number of high-quality decisions," he continued. To make the best decisions possible — as opposed to the greatest number of low-quality decisions, he believes business leaders should focus on getting the sleep they need to promote cognitive health.

Research backs this up. Berkeley neuroscientist Matthew Walker and his team have peered into the human brains to test emotional processing, memory, and learning, decision-making. They found the lack of sleep can prevent us from forming new memories. Walker explains, "Without sleep, the memory inbox shuts down, and you can't commit new experiences to memory. So, those incoming informational emails are bounced, and you end up feeling you are amnesic." Furthermore, the lack of sleep can lead to developing a toxic protein in the brain called beta-amyloid, which has been associated with Alzheimer's disease. On the other hand, deep sleep washes away this toxic protein, which prevents Alzheimer's disease.

Good leaders should promote a "sleep-friendly" organization. If you as a leader, show you are always available 24/7, you are not setting a good example. Be a role model and show them how well-rested you are before you show up for the work. Some jobs require working late nights in shifts but give employees enough time to sleep well before they show up for work the next day. By doing this, you will find your team is more productive, and they will produce quality results. Some organizations even encourage their employees to rest and recharge at work. Notable among them are Google, NASA, Samsung, Uber, Ben & Jerry's, and Zappos. If you can't do that, at least accommodate their unexpected schedule and consider flexible hours. Sometimes, due to personal reasons, your employee might not have slept well. Be flexible with them, and they will go the extra mile for you and your customers. After all, you want them to give you their best hours of the day, don't you?

Exercise to help build your leadership fitness.

In today's fluid and an agile business environment characterized by "just-in-time" planning, the ability to make the correct decision at a moment's notice is very important. You might have planned well in advance, but the newest and best information is available right now! The only tool to keep your ax sharp amid demanding and stressful jobs is to keep your mind and body fit.

You don't have to be an athlete or get involved in bodybuilding if you are not interested. Simple aerobic exercise that suits your lifestyle is just fine. Aerobic means "with oxygen." During aerobic activities, your breathing and heart rate will increase. This can be thirty minutes running on the treadmill or outdoors, spinning, swimming, walking, hiking, dancing, skiing, or kickboxing — whatever you enjoy and doesn't feel like a chore to you. A study by the University of British Columbia shows that aerobic exercise gets the blood flowing and enables the hippocampus to grow, boosting verbal learning and memory skills.

Exercise and aerobic activities also increase the health of our body's microbiome. Regular exercise can reduce insulin resistance and inflammation, and stimulate the release of growth chemicals. These growth chemicals in the brain affect the health of brain cells and new blood vessels, and help new brain cells survive. The deep limbic system is a subsystem of the brain primarily responsible for mood control. When this part of the brain isn't working correctly, we tend to experience moodiness and negativity. According to brain scientists and doctors, aerobic exercises can help activate this area of the brain to swiftly help restore your mood.

Leaders who maintain their physical fitness demonstrate to their employees they can set personal goals and hold themselves accountable. When you care about your physical and mental wellbeing, you demonstrate to your team and organization you already have the qualities of a great leader — self-discipline, accountability, dedication, and the ability to make good decisions. And you'll inspire them to do the same for their bodies and minds.

Finding your "Eureka" moments.

In 287 B.C., the Greek mathematician Archimedes was charged with proving that a new crown made for Hieron, the king of Syracuse, was not pure gold as the goldsmith had claimed. This was an unsolved problem at that time. It kept Archimedes up several nights, tossing and turning in his bed. Finally, his equally exhausted wife convinced him to take a bath to relax. Deep in thought, pondering how best to solve the king's problem, he noticed as he began to lower himself into the tub that the water started to spill out over the sides. What happened next is history.

Had Archimedes not seen water spill out from a bathtub before? Had Newton not seen a falling object before he discovered gravity? While solving a unique and complex problem, the mind can get stuck in the same pathway of thinking again and again. When you continuously work on a new problem, you can become fixated on previous solutions instead of thinking outside the box. Taking a short break from the problem and focusing on something else gives the mind some time to release its hang-up on the same solutions. Some people go for a walk or jog. Some people juggle various projects at the same time while their conscious mind is focusing on one project. Others let their unconscious mind work out a problem. The key is to put yourself in a position to seize these Eureka moments by looking at the world, and the problems you're trying to solve, with fresh eyes and an agile mind.

Leading with the soul and bringing spirit to your organization.

Executives have begun to understand that to build a great business, companies need a larger goal and a broader purpose. This is essential to attract the best and brightest talents today. People want to be passionate about what they do, and they want to be surrounded by people who are equally passionate. According to James Whitehurst, former IBM President and Red Hat CEO, "The challenge for leaders is that there is no formal management theory for how to build, leverage, and measure the level of passion in your employees. It primarily falls into that ambiguous category of 'you'll know it when you see it.'" Leaders can start by acknowledging that soul and spirit are intimately connected. Leaders with a sound soul bring the right spirit to the organization, and they can transform their workplace into a community with passion and purpose. Every company today has some mission statement, and they communicate it effectively, but not every company relays their purpose and shows their passion. In a workplace, when employees do good, they feel good. When they don't get the desired results, they may feel inadequate, angry, or frustrated. And that's okay! Emotional intelligence is not about masking emotions. Let your employees show their emotions. If you ask your employees to check their emotions (good or bad) at the door of the workplace, you won't be able to tap into their passion.

Integrating spirit in your workplace begins with the leader's mindset shift and the hiring of passionate people. Passion is an intrinsic drive of your soul. If you are deeply passionate about something that you enjoy, even if it's a hobby unrelated to work, it can make you a better leader. I know what you are thinking. You have enough work to fill every hour of every day, so where is the time for such things? There is always something more important to attend to. But consider this: life is a journey, and your work or business is a part of it. You cannot know everything going to happen before it happens. In a recent study detailed in *Harvard Business Review*, researchers looked at CEOs of S&P 500 companies and found that only 56 of them had a serious hobby they have a long-term commitment to. Those CEOs stated that their leisure interests help them cope with the ever-increasing demands of the top job, provide detachment, create an atmosphere for continually striving for self-improvement, and create deeper connections with their followers. When involved in such activities that ignite your soul, you provide not only a powerful expression of your values but also a strong identity as a leader. If you lead with a soul, you will leave behind a legacy, not just a business.

Mindful exercises for deliberate and intuitive leadership

Mindfulness is a deliberate practice in which you focus on being intensely aware of what you're sensing and feeling in the moment, without interpretation or judgment. This promotes an understanding of the difference between thinking and awareness—this awareness is called consciousness. Consciousness is a product of the brain and without consciousness, we are just biological robots.

The practice of mindful leadership will give you tools to manage your life as you're living it. You will develop an ability to pay attention to the present moment, recognizing your emotions, and keeping them under control. There has been much neuroscientific research over the past two decades that proves mindfulness not only changes the function of the brain but also changes its physical structure of the brain—a finding with profound implications.

As I mentioned earlier, about 70,000 thoughts pass through an average adult's brain in a single day, and our minds wander, on average, 47% of the time. In neuroscience, Default Mode Network (DMN), also known as "Task-Negative Network," is a network of interacting brain regions highly correlated with one another and distinct from other networks in the brain. This brain network is negatively correlated with other part of the brain, such as attention networks. Neuroscientists believe the default mode network is most commonly active when a person is not focused on the outside world, and the brain is at wakeful rest, such as during mind-wandering (or daydreaming). According to brain research conducted by Kathleen Garrison at the Yale School of Medicine, meditation is associated with reduced activation of the DMN. Since meditation involves maintaining attention to immediate experience and ignoring distractions, it can help control mind wandering. Scientific research in the area of mindfulness suggests that meditation sharpens emotional intelligence, attention, and memory. Meditation also builds resilience. Multiple studies have shown meditation can decrease anxiety and increase the ability to perform under stress.

Let's consider another problem. As I have mentioned in the previous chapter (Building Adaptive Resilience), many CEOs and executives have a particular problem: they have excessive anxiety and conflict-avoidance tendencies. Dr. Daniel Amen and his crew have done over 160,000 brain scans. After looking at several CEOs' and executives' brain scans, he found that the reason for their level of intense emotion and conflict avoidance was due to high "basal ganglia " activities in their brain, as I explained in the previous chapter. Dr. Amen proposes mental exercises and meditation to handle this issue.

Among many studies, the one that shows very clear results of mindfulness-based stress reduction was conducted by [26]Dr. Goldin and team at Stanford University. They are well-known neuroscientists for their research in cognitive-affective neuroscience, emotion, and emotion regulation. Compared with baseline, those who employed mindfulness techniques showed improvement in symptoms of anxiety, depression, and self-esteem symptoms. During the breath-focused attention task, the researchers also found several positive results: increased activity in brain regions associated with attentional deployment, decreased negative emotion experience, reduced

---

[26] Dr. Philippe Goldin, associate professor at UC Davis, and James Gross, professor at Stanford University and the director of the Stanford Psychophysiology Laboratory.

amygdala activity (the amygdala is responsible for negative emotions such as anger, fear, sadness, and aggression).

The Power of Breath and Meditation

We can't completely eliminate stress from our work or life, but we can make ourselves better able to process the stress and neutralize it. Breath work is the most time efficient stress reduction tool, and the results are long lasting. If you think about it, breathing is the only body function you can do either completely consciously or completely unconsciously. Therefore, it allows an open channel between the conscious mind and the unconscious mind. Breath is a true connection between mind, body, and soul. Perhaps that's why in many languages and in many spiritual traditions, the word for breath and spirit is the same: *"Prana"* in Hindi language means breath and spirit. Likewise, in Hebrew, the word for both is the same; it's called *"Ruach."* The Greek word for spirit is *"Pneuma"*, which also means breath. In Chinese, the words used for breath and soul are *"Chi"* or *"Qi."*

A study carried out by Rochester University found that, despite our brain comprising only two percent of the body, it consumes twenty percent of oxygen supply. Several studies on slow-breathing techniques consistently suggest their ability to foster positive emotions and behaviors, facilitating emotional regulation and overall well-being. In the audio version of this book, I have also explained proven breathing exercises that you can practice easily for a few minutes a day. During any mindfulness practice, the safest place to put our attention is on breath. You can also practice breathing slowly during the day or the next time you are stuck in a traffic jam. Try to breathe from your belly instead of shallow breathing.

I have spoken with many executives about their mindfulness experiences. People who practice meditation have greater control over their emotions, develop more mental clarity, and are less likely to react impulsively to unexpected business outcomes. There are various meditation and mindfulness techniques you can incorporate into your life and your workplace. Since these techniques make more sense to follow along in action, I have published that only in the audio version of this book. It's extremely difficult for anyone to sit and have an "empty mind," but by practicing mindfulness, we can become better at quieting our minds. I strongly recommend you should listen and follow the step-by-step mindfulness and meditation techniques. I have explained three meditation techniques to cultivate your emotional intelligence. I have been practicing these techniques for over 20 years and I have found them extremely helpful. You can practice these for ten to fifteen minutes a day. Anyone can gain from these techniques, but these techniques are well suited for busy leaders and executives. With a calm mind, you can find vision, strength, and mental clarity. With these mindfulness practices, you will reclaim your overloaded brain and bring your life back under control. These positive effects will translate readily to your business life, making you a more alert, deliberate, intuitive and empathetic leader.

Mindfulness Exercises that don't Take Time

We can only do so much in a day. For leaders like you, sometimes a workday may be stretched to twelve or even sixteen hours. How can you find time for yourself? You do so many things, and if you don't have time for meditation, mindfulness, or breathing exercises, I have good news for you. There is an alternative. Throughout the day, try to be conscious and deliberate about what you're doing. It is humanly impossible to be deliberate and mindfully conscious about everything. But you can choose a couple of activities you want to completely focus and be mindful of. For example, you can pair hand washing with a simple breathing exercise and mindfulness practice. Take a gentle breath through your nose for five seconds and exhale through your mouth for five seconds. Repeat this a couple of times. Try to focus on every part of hand washing. Mindfulness can be as simple as connecting with your senses during this activity. Listen to the sound of the water from the tap and the other noises around you. Try to smell the fragrance of soap. Notice the feeling of the water and soap on our hands. Try lengthening your inhale and exhale, which eases the mind and body. You can add such mindfulness to another similar activity next week.

Our minds are the most powerful tool we have. The mind, as we have seen, starts with the brain — not just the left and right brain, and not just the "head brain," but our hearts and our guts, as well. Leaders must understand and be role models who treat their bodies, minds, and souls well. Enough sleep, healthy nutrition, proper hydration, regular exercise, and the practice of deep breathing to oxygenate the body and brain have positive, measurable effects on you and your team's performance.

Our physical health has profound effects on our mental well-being. To be a role model for your employees, leaders should commit themselves to exercising, meditating, and becoming resilient to stress. You will find, you will be better equipped to confront any challenge that comes your way, but you'll also inspire your workforce to follow your lead and bring the full potential of their minds, bodies, and souls to the workplace. When you are ready for the mindfulness journey with me, please move forward to the bonus section of this audiobook – *"Mindfulness Practices for Leaders"* read by Debbie Grattan. Some of the techniques described in this section date back to over seven thousand years. I feel honored to present this for busy individuals like you. Whether you're new to mindfulness or you already practice, you may find these very enlightening and easy to follow.

If you use the skills, tools, and techniques described in this book, you will be better equipped to understand where your customer, stakeholders, and employees are coming from and how to lead any complex situation —with or without authority or positional power. **You are as good as the tools you have, and the most powerful tools you have are — your mind and body.** *You knew it all in your heart, I have just tried to share my perspective on these.*

For more information, please visit - **LeadingWithEQ.com**. *I'd love to hear from you. When you are on this website, please click on the "Contact" button to share the feedback or any suggestions you may have. Building business and leadership is a journey—make it your own!*

Author's Notes

What Inspired me to Write this Book

My father was a mathematics professor specializing in mathematical astronomy. I grew up watching him solve complex mathematical and astronomical problems, which fueled my desire to explore how the universe works. That fascination led me to my first job at one of the most reputable space agencies in the world. I created software to monitor and control spacecraft sensors used in the Polar Satellite Launch Vehicle (PSLV). Years after being a computer scientist and problem solver and working with some of the world's leading minds and thought leaders in the world, I slowly matured out of that and entered the world of people. And I realized it's not less challenging than understanding the "macro-world" of the entire universe or the "micro-world "of cutting-edge technologies. That led me to write this book.

Thanks to the past two decades of corporate experience, I've come to understand, predict, and manage human behavior in organizations and businesses. Working with Fortune 500 companies, government agencies, and SMBs gave me a deep insight into a range of corporate culture and employee and customer experience. I have led companies through several successful M&As integration processes and helped build resilient teams. I had the honor to serve as a chairperson of the advisory board for some of the oldest and largest colleges in the United States. As an executive in a technology company, I believe team building and customer service go hand-in-hand—it's all about understanding their unmet and unarticulated needs.

Whether it's writing a book or executing a new project—we can tackle the challenges in the same way. We set goals aligned with our desire. Since I started writing this book, I changed my environment to increase my knowledge and self-belief. I joined a local author group at the city library. I am also honored to serve as the Vice President of this author group.

I have reasoned through this book; Brain health is a critical piece of our overall health and society. It underlies our ability to communicate, decision-making, problem-solving, and living a healthy and happy life. I am donating 100% of my author proceeds for brain health research.

Production Team

I would like to take a moment to thank intelligent individuals who have helped my book along the way. Without their help, I couldn't have done it.

Will (Editing): Editor, copyeditor, and publishing consultant with over ten years of publishing industry experience. He is specialized in business and finance.

Jennifer (Editing): She is a professional editor and writer with a degree in journalism. She is a published author and a member of the American Copy Editors Society.

Miriam (Editing): She has extensive experience in writing, editing, marketing, and business communication.

Troy (Narration): Voice Over Artist, Character Voice Actor, and Storyteller with over 35 years of professional experience in the voice over and multimedia fields.

Debbie (Narration): She has leveraged her acting skills and talents into a very successful career as a professional female voice over talent over the past two decades.

Mahreen (Graphics Design): She is a business IT professional with a passion for creating visually appealing infographics and designing UI/UX that brings aesthetics and customer experience together.

Megan (Graphics Design): She is computer programming and analytics professional ever expanding her experience within the IT world. She enjoys acquiring new skills and finding opportunities to utilize them. Design is one such skill that she is currently taking pleasure in perfecting.

Prashant (Cover Design): A mechanical engineer by profession. He loves sketching, playing basketball, and repairing things on his own. In his spare time, he is either reading a book or designing one.

Dikchhya (Review & Website): Data analytics IT professional. She has an eye for quality assurance with strong attention to detail. Her academic knowledge of organizational psychology was very helpful.

Rik (Book Formatting): He holds a master's degree in Curriculum Design and Teaching. He is a retired educator and has formatted more than 3,000 books since 2012. He lives in eastern Canada with his wife of 50 years and a very spoiled cat.

Continue the leadership journey at:

www.LeadingWithEQ.com

www.ingramcontent.com/pod-product-compliance
Lightning Source LLC
Chambersburg PA
CBHW020840120726
48008CB00004B/74/J